Speak English Like an American

HABLE INGLÉS COMO LOS AMERICANOS

YOU ALREADY SPEAK ENGLISH...
NOW SPEAK IT EVEN BETTER!

DELUXE BOOK & CD SET

AMY GILLETT

LANGUAGE SUCCESS PRESS

ANN ARBOR, MICHIGAN

First Edition

ISBN 0-9725300-1-0
Library of Congress Control Number: 2003091933

Visit our web-site: www.languagesuccesspress.com

Bulk discounts are available. For information, please contact:

Language Success Press
2232 S. Main Street #345
Ann Arbor, MI 48103
USA

E-mail: sales@languagesuccesspress.com
Fax: (303) 484-2004 (USA)

Printed in the United States of America

AGRADECIMIENTOS DE LA AUTORA
Author Acknowledgements

¡GRACIAS!
THANK YOU!

La autora desea agradecerles a las siguientes personas sus consejos y asistencia en la preparación de este libro y CD:
Jacqueline Gillett, Marcy Carreras, Vijay Banta, John McDermott, Natasha McDermott, Cat McGrath, Patrick O'Connell.

The author is very grateful to the following people for their collaboration and advice while preparing this book and CD:
Jacqueline Gillett, Marcy Carreras, Vijay Banta, John McDermott, Natasha McDermott, Cat McGrath, Patrick O'Connell.

LA AUTORA

Amy Gillett ha sido profesora de inglés como segunda lengua en Stamford, Connecticut, y Praga, República Checa. Los ensayos y escritos humorísticos de Amy se han publicado en varias publicaciones nacionales, incluyendo *MAD Magazine*, *The San Francisco Chronicle* y la revista *Family Circle*. Es licenciada en Lenguas y Literaturas Eslavas y tiene un diploma posgraduado en Estudios Rusos, ambos de Stanford University. También ha estudiado en la Universidad Estatal de San Petersburgo.

LA TRADUCTORA

Beatriz Urraca nació en Madrid. Es licenciada en Filología Inglesa por la Universidad Complutense de Madrid y tiene un doctorado en Literatura Comparada de la Universidad de Michigan. Actualmente combina su labor de traducción con la de Profesora Asociada de Español y Humanidades en Neumann College, Pensilvania, y sus publicaciones sobre literatura latinoamericana y norteamericana han aparecido en diversas revistas académicas.

EL ILUSTRADOR

Manny José es ilustrador y diseñador gráfico y lleva tanto tiempo haciendo garabatos y dibujando que ya no recuerda cuánto. Es de Toronto, Canadá y actualmente vive en Brooklyn, Nueva York. Para ver más ilustraciones de Manny, visite www.mannytoons.com.

TABLA DE CONTENIDOS
TABLE OF CONTENTS

INTRODUCCIÓN

Si ya habla algo de inglés y ahora desea hablar más como un nativo, ha encontrado el libro perfecto. Una de las claves para hablar como un nativo es la capacidad de usar y comprender expresiones casuales o modismos. El inglés americano está lleno de modismos. No aprenderá estas expresiones en un libro de texto corriente, pero las oirá constantemente en las conversaciones diarias. También las encontrará en libros, periódicos, revistas y programas de televisión. Este libro le ayudará a entender y utilizar mejor los modismos. Contiene más de 300 de los modismos más comunes hoy en día.

Los modismos le dan color al idioma. Domine los modismos y hablará con menos torpeza, sonará menos como un extranjero. También entenderá más cuando lea y escuche. A menudo los estudiantes de inglés tratan de traducir los modismos palabra por palabra, o literalmente. Si lo hace, acabará preguntándose: "¿Qué querrá decir esto?" Los modismos son difíciles porque funcionan como grupos de palabras, no como palabras individuales. Si se traduce cada palabra por separado, no se aprecia el significado y en muchos casos se acaba con algo que no tiene sentido.

Tomemos como ejemplo uno de los modismos que presentamos en este libro: "out of this world". Esta expresión se usa para describir comida deliciosa. Si usted da una fiesta y sirve un plato delicioso, es posible que su amiga americana le diga: "This paella is out of this world!" Empiece a traducir la expresión palabra por palabra y tendrá que preguntarse: "¿En qué mundo está?" y "¿Por qué me habla de que el paella esté en un mundo, sea el mundo que sea?"

Veamos otro ejemplo. Digamos que usted pertenece a un equipo de tenis. Su equipo ha ganado todos los partidos en seis meses. Usted le podría decir esto a su amigo sin usar un modismo: "Our team is lucky because we keep winning game after game". Esto también se puede expresar con un modismo: "Our team is on a winning streak". Suena mejor, ¿no?

Este libro incluye un CD de todos los diálogos. El CD le ayudará con la pronunciación y también le ayudará a recordar los modismos. Póngalo en casa, en la oficina, en el coche, mientras viaje... en cuanto se dé cuenta, estará hablando inglés como los americanos.

Finalmente, trate de prestar oído a los modismos. Si no sabe lo que significa una expresión, pregúntele a algún amigo. Incorpore los modismos cuando hable y escriba al igual que incorpora vocabulario. Es divertido, y disfrutará mucho más hablando inglés. Como los americanos.

CR

PERSONAJES PRINCIPALES
Main Characters

La autora desea darle las gracias a la familia Johnson por dignarse a aparecer como personajes principales en este libro.

The Johnson Family

Ted (*son*)

Bob (*father*)

Nicole (*daughter*)

Susan (*mother*)

Lesson 1

BOB'S DAY AT WORK

Bob works as a manager in a furniture store. Peter, his boss, is not happy about sales. Bob's new advertising campaign hasn't helped. Peter decides to fire him.

Bob trabaja de encargado en una tienda de muebles. Peter, su jefe, no está satisfecho con las ventas. La nueva campaña publicitaria de Bob no ha ayudado. Peter decide despedirlo.

Peter: Bob, I hate to **break the news**, but our sales were down again last month.

Bob: Down again, Peter?

Peter: Yeah. These days, everybody's shopping at our competition, Honest Abe's Furniture Store.

Bob: But everything in there **costs an arm and a leg**!

Peter: That's true. They do charge **top dollar**.

Bob: And their salespeople are very strange. They really **give me the creeps**!

Peter: Well, they must be doing something right over there. Meanwhile, we're **about to go belly-up**.

Bob: I'm sorry to hear that. I thought my new advertising campaign would **save the day**.

Peter: **Let's face it**: your advertising campaign was a **real flop**.

Bob: Well then I'll **go back to the drawing board**.

Peter: It's too late for that. You're fired!

Bob: What? You're **giving me the ax**?

Peter: Yes. I've already found a new manager. She's as **sharp as a tack**.

Bob: Can't we even **talk this over**? **After all**, I've been working here for 10 years!

Peter: There's **no point in** arguing, Bob. I've already **made up my mind**.

Bob: Oh well, **at least** I won't have to **put up with** your nonsense anymore! Good-bye to you and good-bye to this **dead-end job**.

Peter: Please leave before I **lose my temper**!

IDIOMS – LESSON 1

about to – ready to; on the verge of
a punto de, listo para

EXAMPLE: It's a good thing Bob left the furniture store when he did. Peter was so angry, he was **about to** throw a dining room chair at him.

after all – despite everything; when everything has been considered
después de todo, a pesar de todo

EXAMPLE: You'd better invite Ed to your party. **After all**, he's a good friend.

at least – anyway
por lo menos

EXAMPLE: We've run out of coffee, but **at least** we still have tea.
NOTA: La segunda definición de esta frase es "no menos de": There were **at least** 300 people waiting in line to buy concert tickets.

(to) break the news – to make something known
dar la noticia

EXAMPLE: Samantha and Miguel are getting married, but they haven't yet **broken the news** to their parents.

(to) cost an arm and a leg – to be very expensive
costar mucho, costar un ojo de la cara

EXAMPLE: A college education in America **costs an arm and a leg**.
SYNONYMS: to cost a small fortune; to cost a pretty penny

dead-end job – a job that won't lead to anything else
trabajo sin perspectivas de futuro, trabajo sin futuro

EXAMPLE: Diane realized that working as a cashier was a **dead-end job**.

(let's) face it – accept a difficult reality
aceptar algo difícil, asumirlo

EXAMPLE: **Let's face it**, if Ted spent more time studying, he wouldn't be failing so many of his classes!

(to) give one the creeps – to stir in someone a feeling of disgust or horror
darle repugnancia

EXAMPLE: Ted's friend Matt has seven earrings in each ear and an "I Love Mom" tattoo on his arm. He really **gives Nicole the creeps**.

(to) go back to the drawing board – to start a task over because the last try failed; to start again from the beginning
volver a empezar desde el principio

EXAMPLE: Nobody liked the architect's plan for the house, so he had to **go back to the drawing board**.

(to) go belly-up – to go bankrupt
quedar en bancarrota

EXAMPLE: Many people lost their jobs when Enron **went belly-up**.

(to) give someone the ax – to fire someone
despedir

EXAMPLE: Mary used to talk to her friends on the phone all day, until one day her boss finally **gave her the ax**.
SYNONYMS: to send someone packing; to can someone; to let someone go

(to) lose one's temper – to become very angry
perder la paciencia

EXAMPLE: Bob always **loses his temper** when his kids start talking on the telephone during dinner.
SYNONYMS: to hit the roof; to blow one's top; to blow a fuse

(to) make up one's mind – to reach a decision
decidirse

EXAMPLE: Stephanie couldn't **make up her mind** whether to attend Harvard or Stanford. Finally, she chose Stanford.

no point in – no reason to; it's not worth (doing something)
no hay motivo para, no vale la pena

EXAMPLE: There's **no point in** worrying about things you can't change.

(to) put up with – to endure without complaint
soportar, aguantar

EXAMPLE: For many years, Barbara **put up with** her husband's annoying and obnoxious behavior. Finally, she decided to leave him.

real flop *or* **flop** – a failure
fiasco, fracaso

EXAMPLE: The Broadway play closed after just 10 days – it was a **real flop!**

(to) save the day – to prevent a disaster
impedir un desastre

EXAMPLE: The Christmas tree was on fire, but Ted threw water on it and **saved the day**.

(as) sharp as a tack – very intelligent
muy perspicaz, muy inteligente

EXAMPLE: Jay scored 100% on his science test. He's as **sharp as a tack.**

(to) talk over – to discuss
discutir, hablar de

EXAMPLE: David and I spent hours **talking over** the details of the plan.

top dollar – the highest end of a price range; a lot of money
mucho dinero

EXAMPLE: Nicole paid **top dollar** for a pair of jeans at Banana Republic.

✎ PRACTICE THE IDIOMS

Fill in the blank with the missing word:

1) I can't believe you bought a couch at Honest Abe's. Everything in that store costs an arm and a _____.

   a) foot   b) leg   c) hand

2) After Bob found out that his advertising campaign failed, he wanted to go back to the drawing _____.

   a) board   b) table   c) room

3) When somebody isn't listening to you, there's no ___ in trying to argue with them.

   a) edge   b) tip   c) point

4) José is really smart. He's as sharp as a _____.

   a) tack   b) nail   c) screw

5) The salespeople at Honest Abe's always look angry and never speak to anybody. No wonder they _____ Bob the creeps.

   a) take   b) give   c) allow

6) Bob got fired. He isn't looking forward to _____ the news to his family.

   a) breaking   b) cracking   c) saying

7) Bob thought his new advertisements would bring in lots of customers and save the _____.

   a) morning   b) night   c) day

8) Fortunately, Bob no longer has to put ___ with his stupid boss at the furniture store.

   a) over   b) in   c) up

ANSWERS TO LESSON 1, p. 159

Lesson 2

BOB RETURNS HOME WITH BAD NEWS

Bob tells his wife Susan that he lost his job. Susan suggests that he start his own business.

Bob le dice a su mujer, Susan, que se ha quedado sin trabajo. Susan sugiere que ponga su propio negocio.

Susan: **What's the matter**, dear?

Bob: Susan, I **got canned** today at work.

Susan: But Bob, you were Peter's **right-hand man**!

Bob: Yes, and he **stabbed me in the back**.

Susan: **Keep your chin up**. Maybe he'll **change his mind** and take you back.

Bob: **When pigs fly**! Once he **makes up his mind,** he never changes it. Besides, I **told him off**.

Susan: **Look on the bright side**: you won't have to **set eyes** on Peter ever again.

Bob: **Thank goodness** for that!

Susan: **Hang in there**. I'm sure you won't be **out of work** for long.

Bob: In the meantime, we'll have to **live from hand to mouth**.

Susan: Don't get too **stressed out,** Bob. We'll **make ends meet.**

Bob: I can always get a job at McDonald's as a **last resort.**

Susan: I don't think they're hiring right now.

Bob: If **worse comes to worst,** we can sell our home and move into a tent.

Susan: Let's **think big!** Maybe you can start your own business.

Bob: **Easier said than done!**

IDIOMS – LESSON 2

(to) change one's mind – to alter one's opinion or decision
cambiar de idea

EXAMPLE: Brandon wasn't going to take a vacation this year, but then he **changed his mind** and went to Bora Bora for two weeks.

easier said than done – more difficult than you think
más difícil de lo que parece, del dicho al hecho hay un gran trecho

EXAMPLE: Moving into a new home is **easier said than done.**

(to) get canned [slang] – to lose one's job; to get fired
ser despedido

EXAMPLE: After Chris **got canned,** it took him a year to find a new job.
SYNONYMS: to get sacked; to be given the ax

(to) hang in there – to persevere; to not give up
aguantar un poco más

EXAMPLE: I know you're four games behind, but you can still win the tennis match. Just **hang in there!**

if worse comes to worst – in the worst case
en el peor de los casos

EXAMPLE: Ted's car isn't running well. **If worse comes to worst,** he can take the bus to school.
NOTA: Existe la variación "if worst comes to worst".

(to) keep one's chin up – to stay positive
no desanimarse

EXAMPLE: Even when he was unemployed and homeless, Bill managed to **keep his chin up**.

last resort – the only alternative left; the last solution for getting out of a difficulty
último recurso

EXAMPLE: David was locked out of his house. He knew that as a **last resort**, he could always break a window.

(to) live from hand to mouth – to barely have enough money to survive
vivir al día, tener lo justo para vivir

EXAMPLE: Jenny was earning $5 an hour at McDonald's. She was really **living from hand to mouth**.

(to) look on the bright side – to be optimistic; to think about the positive part
ser optimista, ver el lado bueno de las cosas

EXAMPLE: Dan was upset that his soccer game was canceled. His mother said, "**Look on the bright side**, now you can stay home and watch TV."

(to) make ends meet – to manage one's money so as to have enough to live on
pasar con lo que se tiene, tener suficiente dinero para vivir

EXAMPLE: Kathy wasn't able to **make ends meet** so she had to ask her parents to pay her rent.

(to) make up one's mind – *Vea el capítulo 1*

out of work – unemployed; not working
desempleado

EXAMPLE: Gary was **out of work** for six months before finding a new job.

right-hand man – the most helpful assistant or employee
el empleado más importante, la mano derecha

EXAMPLE: Juan's **right-hand man** helps him make all his decisions.

NOTA: También existe la expresión "right-hand woman" para referirse a una mujer, pero "right-hand man" es más común.

(to) set eyes on – to look at
echar la vista encima

EXAMPLE: Ted was in love from the moment he **set eyes on** Amber.

(to) stab someone in the back – to betray someone
traicionar

EXAMPLE: Jill and Heather were friends, until Heather **stabbed Jill in the back** by stealing her boyfriend.

(to be) stressed out – under severe strain; very anxious
estresado, tenso

EXAMPLE: Joe is so **stressed out** about his job that he can't sleep at night.

(to) tell off – to scold; to tell someone in strong words what one really thinks
regañar

EXAMPLE: When Ted showed up for chemistry class a half an hour late, his teacher really **told him off**.
SYNONYM: to give someone a piece of one's mind

---

thank goodness – I'm grateful; I'm relieved
gracias a Dios

EXAMPLE: When Ted came home at 4 a.m. last Sunday, his mother said, "**Thank goodness** you're home! I was so worried about you."
SYNONYMS: thank God; thank heaven

(to) think big – to set high goals
crearse objetivos ambiciosos

EXAMPLE: Why run for Governor of New York? **Think big**: run for President of the United States!

What's the matter? – What's the problem?
¿qué pasa?

EXAMPLE: **What's the matter**, Bob? You don't look very happy.
SYNONYM: What's wrong?

---

when pigs fly [slang] – never
nunca

EXAMPLE: Will Ted teach Nicole how to play the guitar? **When pigs fly**!
SYNONYMS: when hell freezes over; never in a million years

✎ PRACTICE THE IDIOMS

Fill in the blank with the missing word:

1) What's the _____? You look upset.

   a) situation   b) issue   c) matter

2) I know I can trust you. You would never stab me in the _____.

   a) leg   b) back   c) arm

3) If Bob and Susan run out of money, they can always borrow money from Susan's sister as a ____ resort.

   a) final   b) first   c) last

4) You look really stressed ____. Why don't you sit down, relax, and have a cup of tea?

   a) about   b) in   c) out

5) Bob, everything will be fine. You just need to keep your chin ____ and remember that tomorrow is another day.

   a) up   b) down   c) above

6) I just can't make up my ____ whether to order chicken or fish.

   a) head   b) brain   c) mind

7) Nicole accidentally stepped on Ted's guitar. Ted got really angry and told her ____.

   a) off   b) out   c) away

8) Your husband left you for his psychologist? Hang __ there! I'm sure he'll realize she's crazy and then come back to you.

   a) up   b) in   c) out

ANSWERS TO LESSON 2, p. 159

Ted's chemistry class is way over his head.

Lesson 3

TED'S DAY AT SCHOOL

Ted tells his parents he did poorly on his chemistry test. They tell him he needs to get serious and study more.

Ted les dice a sus padres que el examen de química le salió mal. Ellos le dicen que necesita ponerse a estudiar en serio.

Susan: How was your day at school today, Ted?

Ted: Bad. I had a chemistry test, and I **blew it**!

Susan: Maybe if you didn't **cut class** so often, you'd do better.

Bob: That's right, son. Stop **slacking off** and start **hitting the books**!

Ted: But I **can't stand** chemistry class. Besides, it's a **lost cause**. That class is way **over my head**.

Susan: You need to **buckle down**.

Ted: When I'm a famous musician, people won't **give a hoot** about my knowledge of atoms and molecules.

Bob: That's **beside the point.**

Susan: We know you have your **heart set on** going to New York University.

Bob: And you don't **stand a chance** of getting in there with such poor grades!

23

IDIOMS – LESSON 3

beside the point – not relevant
no importa

EXAMPLE: Whether or not I asked the waiter to bring us water is **beside the point**. Waiters should always bring water to the table.

(to) blow something – to spoil or botch something
fallar, estropear

EXAMPLE: Sharon **blew the interview** and didn't get the job offer.

(to) buckle down – to start working seriously
aplicarse, dedicarse con empeño

EXAMPLE: If Jason **buckles down** now, he might be able to graduate from high school this year.

can't stand – to hate
no poder soportar

EXAMPLE: Bob **can't stand** bureaucrats, so he'd never do well working at a large corporation.

(to) cut class – to miss class without an excuse
faltar a clase

EXAMPLE: Ted often **cuts class** to spend more time with his girlfriend.

Get real! – be serious or realistic about what's going on
Sé realista, no seas iluso, ¿en qué mundo vives?

EXAMPLE: You think you won't get a speeding ticket when you drive 85 miles per hour? **Get real!**

(to) have one's heart set on – to really want something
tener la esperanza puesta en, desear algo intensamente

EXAMPLE: Nicole **has her heart set on** studying in Madrid during college.

(to) hit the books – to start studying
empezar a estudiar

EXAMPLE: Ted partied all weekend. Finally, on Sunday night, he decided it was time to **hit the books**.

lost cause – something hopeless
causa perdida

EXAMPLE: Cindy spent five years studying Japanese. Finally, she realized it was a **lost cause**. She would never learn it.

(to) not give a hoot – to not care about
no importarle, no importarle un comino

EXAMPLE: Tom likes to walk around town in his pajamas — he doesn't **give a hoot** what people think.

SYNONYMS: to not give a damn [grosero]; to not give a darn

---

over one's head – beyond one's understanding
no entender nada

EXAMPLE: The article on cloning was written for scientists. It was **over my head**.

(to) slack off – to waste time
perder el tiempo

EXAMPLE: Amanda doesn't get much done at the office. She's too busy **slacking off**.

NOTA: "Slack off" también significa disminuir o reducir la intensidad o velocidad.

(to) stand a chance – to have the possibility of success
tener posibilidades de éxito

EXAMPLE: Although the American figure skaters were good, they didn't **stand a chance** of winning a gold medal at the Olympics.

✎ PRACTICE THE IDIOMS

Choose the most appropriate reply to the following statements:

1) *Bob:* "Susan, I can't get my old job back. It's a lost cause."
   Susan's reply:
   a) "Lost? Maybe I can help you find it."
   b) "Yes, I know it's not a good cause."
   c) "I understand. You'll find something else."

2) *Susan:* "How could Peter fire you? Were you slacking off?"
   Bob's reply:
       a) "No. I was working very hard!"
       b) "No. I talked on the phone to friends all day."
       c) "Yes. I was working very hard!"

3) *Ted:* "It's getting late. I'd better start hitting the books."
   Bob's reply:
       a) "Yes, that's a good idea. Spend some time studying."
       b) "Hit the books? Why don't you read them instead?"
       c) "Why don't you study instead?"

4) *Peter:* "I don't give a hoot how long you've been working here."
   Bob's reply:
       a) "I wouldn't give you a hoot either."
       b) "I guess our years together aren't important to you."
       c) "Yes, it was a long time."

5) *Bob:* "Susan, the truth is that I couldn't stand Peter."
   Susan's reply:
       a) "I know. Peter really liked you too."
       b) "I liked him too. He was a nice guy."
       c) "I didn't like him either. He was a jerk."

6) *Susan:* "Nicole, do you ever cut class?"
   Nicole's reply:
       a) "No. I've never missed a single class."
       b) "Yes. I had to leave my math class early yesterday."
       c) "No. Sometimes I go to the mall during class time."

7) *Bob:* "This book on computers is way over my head."
   Susan's reply:
       a) "Over your head? It should be in front of your face!"
       b) "Why don't you start with an easier book?"
       c) "Here, try this book. It's more difficult."

8) *Nicole:* "I've got my heart set on going to the school picnic."
   Susan's reply:
       a) "Okay. You should definitely go."
       b) "Really? Why don't you want to go?"
       c) "I understand. Picnics can be boring."

ANSWERS TO LESSON 3, p. 159

NICOLE'S DAY AT SCHOOL

Nicole tells her mother Susan about her successful presentation at school. Her brother Ted overhears and interrupts the conversation.

Nicole le cuenta a su madre, Susan, que su presentación en el colegio le salió muy bien. Su hermano Ted la oye por casualidad e interrumpe la conversación.

Susan: How was your day at school today, Nicole?

Nicole: It was great, Mom. I gave a presentation on Hillary Clinton in government class. Afterwards, my teacher **paid me a compliment**.

Susan: What did she say?

Nicole: She said my presentation was **head and shoulders above** the others.

Susan: **Way to go!**

Nicole: She also said I should **go into** politics, just like Hillary.

Ted: You're so **gung ho** about school. It **drives me crazy**.

Nicole: Ted, don't **butt in**! You're just jealous.

Ted: Right. You **hit the nail on the head**. I'm **green with envy**.

Nicole: Would you just **shut up**? You're **on thin ice with** me right now.

Ted: Oh no! Look at me. I'm **shaking in my shoes**!

IDIOMS – LESSON 4

(to) butt in [slang] – to interrupt; to interfere
interrumpir, interferir

EXAMPLE: Sara is rude. She always **butts in** when other people are talking.

NOTA: A menudo verá la expresión "to butt into a conversation". Example: We were talking. Please don't come over and **butt into our conversation**.

(to) drive one crazy – to annoy someone very much
volverle loco, molestar

EXAMPLE: When car alarms go off late at night, it **drives me crazy**.
SYNONYMS: to drive one nuts; to drive one up a wall

(to) go into – to enter a profession
meterse en (una profesión)

EXAMPLE: Lisa enjoys arguing with people, so she decided to **go into** law.

NOTA: "Go into" tiene otros significados:
   1. Entrar en un sitio. **Go into** the house and get a pen.
   2. Ponerse (con estados emocionales). Joe **went into** hysterics.
   3. Discutir detalles. I don't have time now to **go into** the whole story.

green with envy – desiring another's advantages or things
verde de envidia

EXAMPLE: When Daniel got promoted to vice president of the bank, his colleagues were **green with envy**.

gung ho – very enthusiastic
entusiasta, entusiasmado

EXAMPLE: Heather is really **gung ho** about her new job.

head and shoulders above – far superior to
aventajarle en mucho

EXAMPLE: The Boston Symphony Orchestra is **head and shoulders above** any other orchestra in the area.

(to) hit the nail on the head – to be absolutely right
dar en el clavo

EXAMPLE: Dawn **hit the nail on the head** when she said that Tiffany was jealous of Amber.

SYNONYM: to hit the mark

(to be) on thin ice (with someone) – to be in a dangerous position
en una situación comprometida o peligrosa (con alguien)

EXAMPLE: Zachary was **on thin ice** with his mom after he spent his lunch money on candy bars.

(to) pay (someone) a compliment – to give someone a compliment; to offer someone an admiring comment
hacerle un cumplido a alguien

EXAMPLE: Professor Russo **paid Jennifer a compliment**. He said she had a beautiful smile.

(to) shake in one's shoes – to tremble with fear
temblar de miedo

EXAMPLE: Brianna is scared of her French teacher, Monsieur Le Monstre. Whenever he speaks to her, Brianna starts **shaking in her shoes**.

shut up
hay 2 definiciones
1) be quiet, stop speaking
callarse

EXAMPLE: The used car salesman talked on and on. I thought he'd never **shut up**.

2) Stop speaking!
cállate

EXAMPLE: Nicole kept telling Ted to turn down his stereo. Finally, he got angry and said, "**Shut up**!"

NOTA: Recuerde que decirle a alguien "shut up!" es descortés. Mejor diga "Be quiet!" o para ser más cortés "Please be quiet!"

Way to go! – Good work!
¡buen trabajo!

EXAMPLE: You won $2,000 in the poetry writing contest? **Way to go!**

🖎 PRACTICE THE IDIOMS

Fill in the blank with the missing word:

1) Nicole is in a good mood because her teacher _____ her a compliment.

     a) told   b) paid   c) provided

2) Nicole's teacher told her she was ____ and shoulders above her classmates.

     a) elbow   b) neck   c) head

3) When my friend Chad told me he'd just won the lottery, I was ____ with envy.

     a) blue   b) green   c) red

4) When you do something well, your boss might tell you, "Way ____!"

     a) to come   b) to go   c) to act

5) When the robbers entered my house, I was in the kitchen shaking in my _____.

     a) slippers   b) pajamas   c) shoes

6) If somebody is bothering you, you can tell them they're driving you _____.

     a) crazy   b) angry   c) unhappy

7) If you like power, you might consider going ____ politics.

     a) above   b) towards   c) into

8) "You've been yelling and screaming for the past two hours. Could you just shut ___ already?"

     a) up   b) in   c) off

Bonus Practice

Choose the best substitute for the phrase or sentence in bold:

1) When her friend Melissa got into Yale, Nicole was **green with envy**.
   a) sick
   b) happy for her
   c) very jealous

2) Bob and Susan are really **gung ho** about the TV show *Survivor*. They watch it every Thursday night.
   a) enthusiastic
   b) concerned
   c) angry

3) **Shut up!** I can't take any more of your screaming.
   a) Talk louder!
   b) Be quiet!
   c) Get out!

4) You got a scholarship to attend Harvard? **Way to go!**
   a) Too bad!
   b) Good work!
   c) Oh well!

5) Please don't **butt in**! We weren't talking to you.
   a) look at us
   b) disagree with us
   c) interrupt our conversation

6) These cookies aren't very good. I think you **hit the nail on the head** when you said I should add more sugar next time.
   a) were wrong
   b) were right
   c) were confused

ANSWERS TO LESSON 4, p. 159

Lesson 5

TED GOES OUT FOR THE EVENING

Ted leaves to go visit his girlfriend Amber. Ted's mother Susan says she doesn't really like Amber. She wishes him a good time anyway.

Ted se va a visitar a su novia, Amber. La madre de Ted, Susan, dice que a ella no le gusta mucho Amber. De todas formas le desea que se lo pase bien.

Ted: See you later, Mom!

Susan: Where are you going, Ted?

Ted: I told Amber I'd **drop by**.

Susan: What are you two going to do?

Ted: Maybe go to the movies or to a party. Our plans are still **up in the air**.

Susan: Why don't you invite her over here?

Ted: I don't want to **hang around** here. Dad is really **down in the dumps**.

Susan: Is Amber the girl with the nose ring and the purple hair?

Ted: Yeah. I'm **crazy about** her!

Susan: Don't **take this the wrong way**, but she's not exactly my **cup of tea**.

Ted: **Take it easy**, Mom. We're not **about to** get married. We just enjoy **hanging out** together.

Susan: I guess **there's no accounting for taste**. **Have a good time**.

Ted: Don't worry. We'll **have a blast!**

Susan: (**under her breath**) That's what I'm afraid of!

IDIOMS – LESSON 5

about to – *Vea el capítulo 1*

(to be) crazy about – to like very much
loco por

EXAMPLE: Amy is so **crazy about** tennis, she'd like to play every day.

cup of tea – the type of person or thing that one generally likes
no ser de su gusto

EXAMPLE: Hockey is not Alan's **cup of tea**. He prefers soccer.
NOTA: Esta expresión se suele usar de forma negativa. She's **not my cup of tea**. (No es de mi gusto).

(to be) down in the dumps – to feel sad; be depressed
triste, deprimido

EXAMPLE: It's not surprising that **Lisa's down in the dumps**. Princess, the cat she had for twenty years, just died.

(to) drop by – to pay a short, often unannounced visit
ir a ver, pasar a visitar

EXAMPLE: If we have time before the movie, let's **drop by** Bill's house.

(to) hang around – to spend time idly; to linger
quedarse, vaguear

EXAMPLE: We had to **hang around** the airport for an extra six hours because our flight was delayed.

(to) hang out – to spend time (often doing nothing)
pasar tiempo (a menudo sin hacer nada)

EXAMPLE: Ted spent all of last summer **hanging out** by his friend's pool.
NOTA: "Hang out with" significa "hacerle compañía a alguien".

(to) have a blast [slang] – to enjoy oneself very much
pasarlo muy bien

EXAMPLE: Last summer, Nicole **had a blast** backpacking through Europe with some friends.
SYNONYM: to have a ball

(to) have a good time – to enjoy oneself
pasarlo bien, divertirse

EXAMPLE: Marcy and José **had a good time** salsa dancing at Babalu, a nightclub in Manhattan.

take it easy – relax; don't worry
cálmate

EXAMPLE: You lost your keys? **Take it easy**, I'm sure you'll find them.
SYNONYM: chill out [slang]

(to) take something the wrong way – to take offense
tomarse algo a mal

EXAMPLE: Don't **take this the wrong way**, but I liked your hair better before you got it cut.

NOTA: Se suele usar de forma negativa: "Don't take this the wrong way, but…"

there's no accounting for taste – it's impossible to explain individual likes and dislikes
sobre gustos no hay nada escrito

EXAMPLE: Ted likes to put sugar on his spaghetti. I guess **there's no accounting for taste**.

under one's breath – quietly; in a whisper
en voz baja

EXAMPLE: "Amber is strange," muttered Nicole **under her breath**, as Ted was leaving the room.

NOTA: "Mutter" signfica "murmurar". A menudo se usa con "under one's breath", como en el ejemplo anterior.

(to be) up in the air – not yet determined; uncertain
sin decidir, (estar) en el aire (lit.)

EXAMPLE: It might rain later, so our plans for the picnic are still **up in the air**.

✎ PRACTICE THE IDIOMS

Fill in the blank with the missing word:

1) Bob was fired. It's not surprising that he's down ___ the dumps.

   a) at   b) in   c) with

2) Ted thinks Amber is wonderful. He's just crazy ___ her.

   a) about   b) around   c) into

3) "Don't ___ this the wrong way, but I really don't like your girlfriend," said Susan to Ted.

   a) understand   b) put   c) take

4) Ted likes to hang ___ with Amber. She's fun to be with.

   a) on   b) out   c) in

5) Ted decided to go over to Amber's house. He'd promised her he'd drop ___.

   a) by   b) around   c) near

6) Bob and Susan don't know where they'll go on vacation. Their travel plans are still up ___ the air.

   a) around   b) in   c) above

7) Judy muttered something nasty ___ her breath, but I couldn't quite hear it.

   a) about   b) under   c) below

8) Why are you hanging ___ the house on such a beautiful day? You should be outside enjoying the weather.

   a) inside   b) from   c) around

ANSWERS TO LESSON 5, p. 159

 **Review for Lessons 1-5**

Fill in the blank with the missing word:

1) After copying from his friend's paper during the test, Ted was on _____ ice with his chemistry teacher.

    a) thick   b) thin   c) dangerous

2) Ted's teacher hit the _____ on the head. Ted should spend less time playing guitar and more time studying.

    a) tack   b) nail   c) screw

3) I'm not really crazy about my friend's husband. He talks too much, and he never listens to what anybody else is saying. He's just not my cup of _____.

    a) coffee   b) cocoa   c) tea

4) If Ted has his _____ set on going to New York University, he's going to have to buckle down and start studying more.

    a) life   b) brain   c) heart

5) It's not surprising that Nicole gets such good grades. She's as _____ as a tack.

    a) smart   b) sharp   c) clever

6) When Peter _____ his temper, it's very scary. He throws furniture everywhere.

    a) loses   b) finds   c) opens

7) After Jane started hitting the _____, her grades started improving immediately.

    a) work   b) books   c) teachers

8) Nicole said something _____ her breath, but I couldn't hear it. When I asked her to repeat it, she refused.

a) on   b) about   c) under

9) Will Ted ever be the best student in his class? Sure, when _____ fly!

a) sheep   b) goats   c) pigs

10) A positive attitude leads to success. When things get difficult, it's important to keep your _____ up.

a) chin   b) neck   c) head

11) Bob was all stressed _____ because the traffic was making him late for a doctor's appointment.

a) over   b) out   c) up

12) Frank knew that the judge had already decided he was guilty. There was no point ___ arguing with him.

a) in   b) around   c) about

13) Some people think Nicole and Susan are sisters. That really _____ Nicole crazy!

a) does   b) causes   c) drives

14) Ted has been slacking ____ since the first day of high school, so it's not surprising that he's doing so poorly.

a) around   b) off   c) about

15) During the Depression in the 1930's, many families in America were living from hand to _____.

a) arm   b) mouth   c) hand

ANSWERS TO REVIEW, p. 160

SUSAN STAYS HOME AND BAKES COOKIES

Susan decides to cheer up her husband. Bob loves her home-made cookies. Nicole suggests she start a cookie business.

Susan decide animar a su marido. A Bob le encantan sus galletas hechas en casa. Nicole sugiere que ponga su propio negocio de galletas.

Susan: Bob, I baked cookies for you.

Bob: That was so nice of you, dear. You've got a **heart of gold**!

Susan: Go ahead and **pig out**!

Bob: These are delicious!

Susan: I thought they might **cheer you up**. You've been **in a bad mood** lately.

Bob: I guess I have been a little **on edge**. But these cookies are **just what the doctor ordered**!

Nicole: Do I smell cookies?

Susan: Yes, Nicole. **Help yourself**.

Nicole: Yum-yum.* These are **out of this world**. You could **go into business** selling these!

Bob: You could call them Susan's Scrumptious Cookies. You'd **make a bundle**.

Susan: **Good thinking!**

Nicole: Don't forget to **give me credit** for the idea after you're rich and famous!

Susan: You know I always **give credit where credit is due**!

* Yum-yum: se dice cuando algo está delicioso. También se puede decir "mmm, mmm" o "mmm-mmm, good" [qué rico, delicioso].

IDIOMS – LESSON 6

(to) cheer someone up – to make someone happy
alegrar a alguien

EXAMPLE: Susan called her friend in the hospital to **cheer her up**.
NOTA: La expresión "cheer up!" se suele usar para animar a alguien que se siente deprimido ("¡anímate!").

(to) give (someone) credit – to acknowledge someone's contribution
dar mérito

EXAMPLE: The scientist **gave his assistant credit** for the discovery.

(to) give credit where credit is due – to give credit to the person who deserves it
dar mérito cuando se merece

EXAMPLE: I will be sure to thank you when I give my speech. I always **give credit where credit is due**.

(to) go into business – to start a business
poner un negocio

EXAMPLE: Jeff decided to **go into business** selling baseball cards.

good thinking – good idea
buena idea

EXAMPLE: I'm glad you brought an umbrella — that was **good thinking**!

(to) have a heart of gold – to be very kind and giving
ser muy amable y generoso, tener un corazón de oro (lit.)

EXAMPLE: Ed **has a heart of gold** and always thinks of others before himself.

Help yourself – serve yourself
sírvete

EXAMPLE: "**Help yourselves** to cookies and coffee," said Vanessa before the meeting started.
NOTA: Atención a la forma reflexiva: Help *yourself* en singular, help *yourselves* en plural.

(to be) in a bad mood – unhappy; depressed; irritable
de mal humor

EXAMPLE: After her boyfriend broke up with her, Nicole was **in a bad mood** for several days.
SYNONYM: out of sorts

just what the doctor ordered – exactly what was needed
justo lo que se necesita

EXAMPLE: After coming in from skiing, a cup of hot cocoa was **just what the doctor ordered**.
SYNONYM: to hit the spot. Example: This hot cocoa really **hits the spot**!

(to) make a bundle – to make a lot of money
ganar un dineral

EXAMPLE: Bob's friend Charlie **made a bundle** in the stock market and retired at age 45.
SYNONYM: to make a killing

(to be) on edge – nervous; irritable
nervioso

EXAMPLE: Whenever Susan feels **on edge**, she takes several deep breaths and starts to feel more relaxed.

out of this world – delicious
delicioso

EXAMPLE: Mrs. Field's oatmeal raisin cookies are **out of this world**!
SYNONYM: to die for. Example: This pie is so good — it's **to die for**!

(to) pig out [slang] – to eat greedily; to stuff oneself
comer demasiado, comer como un cerdo, ponerse morado

EXAMPLE: Ted **pigged out** on hot dogs and hamburgers at the barbeque and then got a stomachache.

NOTA: Atención al uso de la preposición "on" después del verbo "to pig out". Se puede **pig out on** hotdogs, **pig out on** candy, **pig out on** ice cream.

✍ Practice the Idioms

Choose the best substitute for the phrase or sentence in bold:

1) Thanks for baking cookies for me. **You've got a heart of gold.**
   a) You're a very nice person.
   b) You're a reliable person.
   c) You're very generous with your money.

2) I baked these cookies for you. **Why don't you pig out?**
   a) Please take just one cookie.
   b) Take as many cookies as you like.
   c) Why don't you ever eat my cookies?

3) I know you'll like my cookies since **you've got a sweet tooth.**
   a) your teeth are hurting
   b) you don't like sweet things
   c) you like sweet things

4) **You should go into business selling cookies.**
   a) You should go to the store and buy some cookies.
   b) You should try to get a job baking cookies.
   c) You should start a company that sells cookies.

5) I baked these cookies. **Help yourself!**
   a) Let me get you one!
   b) Take some!
   c) You need to get some help!

6) If you went into business selling these delicious cookies, **you'd make a bundle.**
   a) you'd make many cookies
   b) you'd make a lot of money
   c) you'd make a few dollars

7) **Good thinking!**
   a) That's a good idea!
   b) It's good that you're thinking!
   c) Keep thinking good thoughts!

8) I was thirsty. This iced tea is **just what the doctor ordered.**
   a) exactly what I needed
   b) very healthy for me
   c) exactly what my doctor recommended

ANSWERS TO LESSON 6, p. 160

SUSAN HIRES BOB TO RUN HER BUSINESS

Susan stays up all night thinking about her cookie business. In the morning, she discusses it with Bob. Bob agrees to work for her.

Susan no se acuesta en toda la noche, pensando en su negocio de galletas. Por la mañana, lo discute con Bob. Bob acuerda trabajar para ella.

Bob: You're up **bright and early** this morning, Susan.

Susan: I **didn't sleep a wink**. I was awake all night thinking about the new business.

Bob: Running your own business is lots of work. Are you prepared to **work like a dog**?

Susan: No. But I am prepared to hire *you* to run the business.

Bob: You want *me* to run a cookie business? **Fat chance!**

Susan: Why not?

Bob: **I don't have a clue** about making cookies. I don't even know how to turn the oven on!

Susan: I'll give you a **crash course**.

Bob: Do I have to do the baking?

Susan: No. You'll just manage the business side.

Bob: **Needless to say**, I have **mixed feelings** about working for you.

Susan: I'll be nice. I promise you'll be a **happy camper**.

Bob: Okay. **Let's give it a shot**, boss!

IDIOMS – LESSON 7

bright and early – early in the morning
muy temprano

EXAMPLE: Our plane for Santiago left at 7:30 a.m., so we had to get up **bright and early**.

SYNONYM: at the crack of dawn

crash course – short and intensive instruction
curso acelerado

EXAMPLE: Yesterday, Joan's son sat down with her for a couple of hours and gave her a **crash course** on using the Internet.

fat chance – very little possibility
ni en sueños

EXAMPLE: The boys at school are always laughing at Dana. Will she be invited to the school dance? **Fat chance!**

SYNONYM: No way!

(to) give it a shot – to try something
intentarlo

EXAMPLE: I've never tried to make wine in my bathtub before, but perhaps I'll **give it a shot**.

SYNONYM: to give it a try

NOTA: La expresión "to give it one's best shot" significa "hacer lo posible". I know you're nervous about the interview — just **give it your best shot**.

46

happy camper [slang] – a happy person; a satisfied participant
satisfecho, encantado, más contento que unas castañuelas, más contento que un niño con zapatos nuevos

EXAMPLE: When Linda's passport was stolen in Florence, she was not a **happy camper**.

NOTA: Esta expresión se suele usar de forma negativa.

(to have) mixed feelings – a conflicted response, positive about one aspect and negative about another
ambivalencia

EXAMPLE: When our houseguests decided to stay for another week, I had **mixed feelings**. On the one hand, I enjoyed hanging out with them. On the other hand, I was tired of cooking for them.

---

needless to say – obviously
no hay que decir, huelga decir, obviamente

EXAMPLE: You've got a test tomorrow morning. **Needless to say**, you can't stay out late tonight.

SYNONYM: it goes without saying. Example: You've got a test tomorrow, so **it goes without saying** that you can't stay out late tonight.

(to) not have a clue – to know nothing about
no tener ni idea

EXAMPLE: Bob talks about working at McDonald's, but the truth is he **doesn't have a clue** about making hamburgers.

SYNONYM: to be clueless. Example: When it comes to cooking, Bob **is clueless**.

(to) not sleep a wink – to be awake all night
no poder dormir, no pegar un ojo

EXAMPLE: Ted was so nervous about his chemistry test that he **didn't sleep a wink** the night before.

(to) work like a dog – to work very hard
trabajar mucho, trabajar duro, trabajar a matarse

EXAMPLE: John became an investment banker after college, and now he **works like a dog**.

SYNONYMS: to work one's tail off; to work like a horse; to work one's fingers to the bone

✎ PRACTICE THE IDIOMS

Fill in the blank with the missing word:

1) Bob was surprised to see his wife up _____ and early in the morning.

   a) light   b) bright   c) ready

2) Last week I worked 80 hours. I really worked like a _____.

   a) dog   b) cat   c) squirrel

3) Bob had never baked anything before in his life. He didn't even have a _____ about how to turn the oven on.

   a) hint   b) suggestion   c) clue

4) If you need to learn something quickly, you'd better take a _____ course.

   a) crash   b) fast   c) beginner's

5) Bob wasn't sure he wanted to work for his wife. He had _____ feelings.

   a) nervous   b) mixed   c) confused

6) Jennifer's boss is lousy and her salary is low. She's not a happy _____.

   a) scout   b) tourist   c) camper

7) Bob decided to work for Susan. He figured he'd give it a _____.

   a) shot   b) pop   c) choice

8) Nicole was up all night finishing her Spanish homework. She didn't sleep a _____.

   a) drink   b) blink   c) wink

ANSWERS TO LESSON 7, p. 160

TED FORMS A ROCK BAND

Ted plans to become a successful musician. First, he needs Susan to loan him money for a new guitar. Susan suggests that Ted bake cookies to earn the money.

Ted quiere ser un músico famoso. Primero, necesita que Susan le preste dinero para comprar una guitarra nueva. Susan sugiere que Ted haga galletas para ganarse el dinero.

Susan: You're **in good spirits** today, Ted.

Ted: I've got great news, Mom.

Susan: What is it?

Ted: Amber and I are going to start a rock band!

Susan: **Good for you!**

Ted: Mom, I'm not going to **beat around the bush**. I need to borrow $1,000 for a new guitar.

Susan: Ted, your father and I can't **shell out** that much. We aren't **made of money**.

Ted: You're not? I thought you were millionaires, like Donald and Ivana Trump!*

Susan: Ha ha. This is no time to be a **wise guy**!

Ted: I promise I'll pay you back.

Susan: How?

Ted: We're going to **take the music world by storm** and make lots of money.

Susan: That sounds like a **pipe dream**. Aren't high school rock bands a **dime a dozen**?

Ted: Yeah, but we're different. With my guitar playing and Amber's beautiful voice, we're sure to **make a splash**!

Susan: Well, we're going through **hard times**. You're going to have to work for that $1,000.

Ted: How?

Susan: You can bake cookies.

Ted: I bet Mrs. Clapton never made Eric** bake cookies, but I guess those are **the breaks**.

* Donald Trump es un famoso millonario americano que se hizo rico especulando en bienes raíces. Ivana es su ex-mujer.

** Eric Clapton es un músico y guitarrista muy popular

IDIOMS – LESSON 8

(to) beat around the bush – to avoid getting to the point; to talk around the subject
andarse con rodeos

EXAMPLE: Kathy **beat around the bush** for an hour, then finally told us she needed a ride to Kennedy Airport.

---

dime a dozen – so plentiful as to be nothing special; common
muy abundante

EXAMPLE: There are so many Starbucks coffee shops in Manhattan, they're a **dime a dozen**.
NOTA: En inglés "a dime" es una moneda americana de diez centavos (de muy poco valor).

Good for you! – Good job! Well done!
¡Felicidades!, ¡Buen trabajo!

EXAMPLE: You won $50,000 on the TV game show *Jeopardy*? **Good for you**!

hard times – a time of difficulty
pasarlo mal

EXAMPLE: Since his wife left him for her dentist, Dan has been going through **hard times**.

(to be) in good spirits – happy; in a good mood
de buen humor

EXAMPLE: After she won the tennis tournament, Emily was **in good spirits**.

made of money – very rich
muy rico

EXAMPLE: My neighbor is re-modeling his house to look like Versailles. He doesn't have good taste, but he certainly is **made of money**.

SYNONYMS: rolling in money; rolling in dough; to have money to burn

(to) make a splash – to make a successful début
causar sensación

EXAMPLE: Nicole's beautiful cousin Cecilia from Santo Domingo really **made a splash** at the high school dance.

SYNONYM: to be a (real) hit. Example: Nicole's cousin Cecilia **was a real hit** at the dance. All the boys wanted to dance with her!

(to) pay (someone) back – to repay a loan or debt
devolver

EXAMPLE: Nicole **paid her friend back** the $10 she borrowed.

NOTA: "Pay back" también quiere decir "vengarse". Example: I know you're the one who stole my car, and one day I'll think of a way to **pay you back**!

pipe dream – an unrealistic hope
ilusión, castillos en el aire

EXAMPLE: Susan would like to move to New Zealand and write romance novels, but she knows that's just a **pipe dream**.

(to) shell out – to pay (often more than one would like)
pagar (normalmente más de lo que uno quiere)

EXAMPLE: Bob **shelled out** $5,000 for Nicole's piano lessons before she decided she'd rather play the flute.

(to) take (something) by storm – to win popularity quickly
popularizarse rápidamente

EXAMPLE: The play "The Producers" really **took New York by storm**.

the breaks – when something bad happens and you can't do anything about it
qué se le va a hacer

EXAMPLE: By the time we got to the theater, the new Harry Potter movie was already sold out. Oh well, that's **the breaks**!

wise guy [slang] – a smart aleck; one who makes a lot of sarcastic comments
insolente

EXAMPLE: When Mrs. Smith asked Tyler what he wanted to be when he grew up, he said, "An adult." She told him not to be such a **wise guy**.

SYNONYMS: wise ass [grosero], smart ass [grosero]

✎ PRACTICE THE IDIOMS

Choose the best substitute for the phrase in bold:

1) I'm **in good spirits** today because I got a promotion at work.
   a) happy
   b) drunk
   c) tired

2) Renting an apartment on Park Avenue in Manhattan is difficult, unless you're **made of money**.
   a) wealthy
   b) strange
   c) famous

3) My friend's daughter paints beautiful pictures. In a few years, **she'll take the art world by storm**.
   a) something bad will happen and she'll lose her job
   b) she'll do an excellent painting of a storm
   c) she'll become a very successful artist

4) Susan thinks that Ted's plan to become a famous rock star is **a pipe dream**.
   a) something that is not likely to happen
   b) Ted's biggest hope
   c) something very realistic

5) If you're looking for a new suit, you shouldn't have a problem. Clothing shops in this town are **a dime a dozen**.
   a) hard to find
   b) everywhere
   c) lousy

6) Ted performed at his high school dance. He knew he'd **made a splash** when all the girls started singing along.
   a) done something wrong
   b) made a very positive impression
   c) created waves

7) Being **a wise guy** can be fun, but it might not make you popular with your teachers.
   a) a very intelligent person
   b) an obnoxious person who makes sarcastic comments
   c) a person whom everybody admires

8) Nicole wants to attend Yale, but her parents don't want to **shell out** $100,000 for the tuition.
   a) waste
   b) save
   c) pay

ANSWERS TO LESSON 8, p. 160

NICOLE FOR PRESIDENT!

Nicole discusses her plans to run for student body president. Nicole wants Ted to ask his friends to vote for her. Ted agrees, in exchange for Nicole's help with his homework.

Nicole discute sus planes de presentarse a las elecciones para presidente del alumnado. Nicole quiere que Ted les pida a sus amigos que voten por ella. Ted está de acuerdo, a cambio de que Nicole le ayude con sus deberes.

Nicole: I've decided to run for student body president! If I'm going to become a senator one day, I should **get some experience under my belt** now.

Ted: Andrea Jenkins is also running. She'll give you a **run for your money**!

Nicole: Andrea Jenkins is an idiot. I'm **by far** the better candidate.

Ted: Don't be so **full of yourself**! I might vote for Andrea.

Nicole: Stop **kidding around. Let's get down to business**. I need your help.

Ted: You want *me* to help *you*?

Nicole: Yes. I need you to **talk** your friends **into** voting for me.

Ted: But you never **give my friends the time of day**. All you give them is the **cold shoulder**.

Nicole: That's because they've got blue hair and nose rings!

Ted: They're better than your friends — a bunch of **goody goodies** and **brown-nosers**!

Nicole: That's **beside the point**. Let's talk about *your* friends and *their* votes.

Ted: Okay. **You scratch my back and I'll scratch yours**. If you do my chemistry homework, I'll help you get the votes.

Nicole: I'm not **crazy about** that idea. But, okay, **it's a deal**. I hope I can **count on you**.

IDIOMS – LESSON 9

beside the point – *Vea el capítulo 3*

brown-noser [slang] – a person who's constantly trying to win favor with people above them, such as teachers or bosses
persona que trata de halagar excesivamente a su jefe o profesor

EXAMPLE: Amanda is such a **brown-noser**. She's always telling her teacher how much she enjoys class.

NOTA: Atención a la forma verbal "to brown-nose". Stop trying to **brown-nose** our teacher all the time. It's driving me crazy!

by far – by a wide margin; by a great difference
con mucho

EXAMPLE: Some people think Tom Hanks is **by far** the best actor in America today.

SYNONYMS: by a long shot; far and away; hands down

(to) count on someone – to depend or rely on someone
contar con alguien

EXAMPLE: My brother has a great sense of humor, so I can always **count on him** to cheer me up.

(to be) crazy about – *Vea el capítulo 5*

---

full of oneself – to think too much of oneself
arrogante

EXAMPLE: After Angela appeared on the cover of *Vogue* magazine, she was really **full of herself**.

SYNONYM: to think oneself hot stuff. Example: Cara won the employee of the month award, and now she **thinks she's hot stuff**.

(to) get down to business – to get serious about a task
manos a la obra, ponerse a la obra

EXAMPLE: The book club members spent the first two hours of their meeting eating and drinking before finally **getting down to business**.

SYNONYM: to get cracking

(to) get *or* to have under one's belt – to achieve *or* to have experience
tener o conseguir experiencia

EXAMPLE 1: Tanya had three years of working for a large law firm **under her belt** before leaving to start her own firm.
EXAMPLE 2: Jim needs to get an MBA **under his belt** to get the job he wants.

(to) give someone a run for his money – to be strong competition
darle a alguien una competencia fuerte

EXAMPLE: We lost the soccer tournament, but we certainly **gave the girls from Stamford High School a run for their money**.

(to) give someone the cold shoulder – to be cold to someone on purpose; to snub someone
volverle la espalda a alguien, tratarle con frialdad

EXAMPLE: When Lisa saw Amber at the mall, she didn't even stop to talk to her. She really **gave her the cold shoulder**.

SYNONYM: To blow someone off. Example: Amber can't understand why Lisa **blew her off** at the mall.

(to not) give someone the time of day – to ignore someone; to refuse to pay any attention to someone
no dirigirle a alguien la palabra, ignorar

EXAMPLE: Megan never **gave me the time of day** back in high school, but now she calls me all the time for advice.

goody goody – self-righteously or annoyingly good
santurrón

EXAMPLE: **Goody goodies** usually sit in the front row and smile at the teacher during class.

SYNONYMS: teacher's pet. Example: Nicole always does her homework on time and gets A's on all her papers. No wonder she's the **teacher's pet**!

it's a deal – I agree (to a proposal or offer)
trato hecho

EXAMPLE: You'll make dinner every night for a month if I help you with your homework? Okay, **it's a deal**!

SYNONYM: you're on. Example: You'll give me a massage if I take out the garbage? **You're on**!

(to) kid around – to joke around; to tease
bromear

EXAMPLE: Jeremy loves to **kid around**, so don't be offended by anything he says.

SYNONYM: to horse around. Example: While they were **horsing around**, Tammy accidentally poked Derek in the eye. He had to be rushed to the emergency room of the hospital.

(to) talk into – to persuade; to convince
convencer

EXAMPLE: Chris didn't want to jump out of the plane, but Erin **talked him into it**.

you scratch my back and I'll scratch yours – if you do me a favor, I'll do you a favor; let's cooperate
cooperar

EXAMPLE: I'll help you with your homework if you do the dishes. **You scratch my back and I'll scratch yours**.

✒ PRACTICE THE IDIOMS

Fill in the blank with the missing word:

1) Nicole is very reliable. You can always count ____ her.

   a) in   b) on   c) with

2) I need to ask you for your help, and I'll do something nice for you in return. You scratch my ____ and I'll scratch yours.

   a) back   b) neck   c) foot

3) Stop kidding ____! Tell me where you hid my shoes.

   a) about   b) around   c) into

4) I can't believe that Jennifer gave you the ____ shoulder. I thought you two were friends.

   a) hot   b) freezing   c) cold

5) Ted's friends didn't want to vote for Nicole, but Ted talked them ____ it.

   a) into   b) around   c) for

6) Although Jim Greene was ____ far the more qualified candidate, he lost the election because of a scandal.

   a) way   b) in   c) by

7) Denise is really full ___ herself. She thinks she's the smartest and most beautiful woman in the world.

   a) with   b) of   c) in

8) Nicole thinks that Andrea is a snob. She says Andrea won't ____ her the time of day.

   a) give   b) allow   c) tell

ANSWERS TO LESSON 9, p. 160

BOB VISITS THE VILLAGE MARKET

Bob goes to the Village Market, a supermarket in town. He asks Carol, the owner of the store, if she would like to sell Susan's Scrumptious Cookies. Carol agrees, but isn't able to tell Bob how much she'll pay him.

Bob va al Village Market, un supermercado del pueblo. Le pregunta a Carol, la dueña del supermercado, si desea vender Susan's Scrumptious Cookies. Carol está de acuerdo, pero no le puede decir a Bob cuánto le va a pagar.

Bob: Thank you for **making time for** me today, Carol.

Carol: **Don't mention it,** Bob. **What's up**?

Bob: My wife baked these cookies **from scratch**. Please take one.

Carol: Mmmm, chewy. These are **out of this world**!

Bob: My wife's a great cook.

Carol: **You can say that again**. I don't want to **make a pig of** myself, but let me take a few more.

Bob: *Oink oink!* **Just kidding!**

Carol: I'd like to sell these at the Village Market. My customers will **go nuts** over these!

Bob: How much would you pay us for each cookie?

Carol: I'm not sure. I need to **roll up my sleeves** and **figure out** the finances.

Bob: Can you give me a **ballpark figure** now?

Carol: I don't want to **jump the gun**. **Sit tight** for now, and we'll **talk things over** this evening.

IDIOMS – LESSON 10

ballpark figure – an approximation
cifra aproximada

EXAMPLE: The auto mechanic didn't know exactly how much the repairs would cost, but he was able to give me a **ballpark figure**.

Don't mention it! – you're welcome
de nada

EXAMPLE: "Thanks for bringing the cookies," I said to Susan. "**Don't mention it!**" she replied.

(to) figure out – to solve; to determine
calcular, resolver

EXAMPLE: Ted couldn't **figure out** one of his math problems, so he asked his sister for help.

from scratch – from the beginning; using all fresh ingredients rather than using a prepared mix
desde el principio, desde cero, casero, usando ingredientes frescos en vez de ya preparados

EXAMPLE 1: The house was in such bad shape, they decided to tear it down and re-build it **from scratch**.

EXAMPLE 2: Did you make these delicious scones **from scratch**?

(to) go nuts [slang] – to react with great enthusiasm
reaccionar con entusiasmo

EXAMPLE: When Tiger Woods got a hole-in-one during the golf tournament, the crowd **went nuts**.

NOTA: Esta expresión también significa "volverse loco".

(to) jump the gun – to start doing something too soon
precipitarse

EXAMPLE: Nicole really **jumped the gun** by writing her acceptance speech before the results of the elections were announced.

---

just kidding – talking more to get a laugh than anything
de broma

EXAMPLE: "Are you sure that's your boyfriend? I thought he was your grandfather. **Just kidding!**"

NOTA: Esta expresión se suele usar después de un chiste o comentario que pueda ofender, como en el ejemplo anterior.

(to) make a pig of oneself [slang] – to overeat; to eat too much
comer demasiado, comer como un cerdo, ponerse morado

EXAMPLE: The apple pie was so delicious, I **made a pig of myself** by eating four slices.

(to) make time for – to put time in one's schedule for something
encontrar el tiempo para

EXAMPLE: Alex is a busy lawyer, but he always **makes time for** his family.

---

out of this world – *Vea el capítulo 6*

(to) roll up one's sleeves – to prepare to work
ponerse a trabajar

EXAMPLE: Let's **roll up our sleeves** and finish making these cookies!

(to) sit tight – to wait patiently
esperar con paciencia

EXAMPLE: Nicole won't hear back from colleges until early April. For now, she'll just have to **sit tight**.

(to) talk over – *Vea el capítulo 1*

What's up? – What's going on? What's new?
¿qué pasa?

EXAMPLE: "**What's up?** I haven't spoken to you in a long time."

---

you can say that again – I absolutely agree with you
bien puede usted decirlo, estar de acuerdo

EXAMPLE: You think our house needs repairs? **You can say that again** — even our toilet is broken!

✑ PRACTICE THE IDIOMS

Imagine that you are Bob and that you're meeting with Carol from the Village Market to sell her your cookies. Choose the most appropriate replies to Carol's questions and statements:

Imagínese que usted es Bob y que tiene una reunión con Carol del Village Market para venderle sus galletas. Escoja las respuestas más apropiadas a las preguntas y afirmaciones de Carol:

1) *Carol:* "I'm glad I was able to make time to see you today."
   Bob's reply:
   a) "I guess I'll see you tomorrow then."
   b) "It must be nice to have so much free time."
   c) "Yes, thanks for fitting me into your busy schedule."

2) *Carol:* "What's up?"
   Bob's reply:
   a) "Fine, thank you."
   b) "I'd like to discuss a business deal with you."
   c) "I don't know. Let me check with my wife."

3) *Carol:* "These cookies are out of this world. What do you think?"
   Bob's reply:
   a) "I agree. They're delicious!"
   b) "I don't know where they are."
   c) "No thanks. I've already had ten cookies."

4) *Carol:* "Did your wife make these from scratch?"
   Bob's reply:
   a) "No, she made them from flour, eggs, and sugar."
   b) "Yes, she did. She loves to bake."
   c) "Yes. She bought a roll of Pillsbury frozen dough and heated it in the oven for 15 minutes."

5) *Carol:* "I ate six cookies. Do you think I've made a pig of myself?"
   Bob's reply:
   a) "Not at all. These cookies are hard to resist!"
   b) "Yes. You look just like a pig."
   c) "Yes. Pigs love to eat cookies too."

6) *Carol:* "I think my customers will go nuts over these cookies."
   Bob's reply:
      a) "I agree. After all, they're very good!"
      b) "Nuts? Sure, we can put nuts in the cookies."
      c) "I disagree. They'll probably like them."

7) *Carol:* "Bob, I'm not ready to give you a ballpark figure yet."
   Bob's reply:
      a) "Okay, how about one dollar per cookie?"
      b) "When you're ready, we can sell them in the ballpark."
      c) "Okay, I can wait until tomorrow."

8) *Carol:* "I don't want to jump the gun by discussing details now."
   Bob's reply:
      a) "I understand. Take some time to think about it."
      b) "I didn't say anything about selling you guns."
      c) "Thanks, I'd love an answer right now."

ANSWERS TO LESSON 10, p. 160

Review for Lessons 6-10

Choose the best substitute for the phrase in bold:

1) This apple pie is **out of this world**.
      a) not bad
      b) from another planet
      c) delicious

2) Jane was feeling **on edge**, so she went to a day spa to relax.
      a) anxious
      b) relaxed
      c) angry

3) You ate 15 cookies? You really **made a pig of yourself**!
      a) turned into an animal with a snout and tail
      b) made yourself sick
      c) ate more than you should have

4) Bob wasn't sure he wanted to work for his wife's cookie company, but she **talked him into it**.
   a) forced him
   b) convinced him
   c) asked him

5) Nancy **doesn't have a clue** about the Internet. She's never even used e-mail.
   a) understands deeply
   b) knows nothing
   c) is learning a lot

6) Stop **beating around the bush**! I don't know what you're trying to tell me.
   a) avoiding the subject
   b) hitting the trees
   c) repeating yourself

7) Paul likes to draw silly cartoons of his classmates on the blackboard before class. He's a **wise guy**.
   a) bad student
   b) smart person
   c) sarcastic person

8) Tom needed to learn how to ride a horse before his trip to Ireland, so he took a **crash course.**
   a) short, intensive class
   b) class in falling down
   c) semester-long class

9) Laura **made a bundle** when she was younger, and now she spends every day on the golf course.
   a) had a good job
   b) made lots of money
   c) stole money

10) The doctor will be with you soon. Please **sit tight**.
   a) come back later
   b) wait patiently
   c) follow me

CROSSWORD PUZZLE

Across

2. Stop beating around the ___ and get to the point already!
6. Susan's cookies really made a ____ at the Village Market. Everybody loved them!
7. You want to be a famous painter? That sounds like a ____ dream!
8. When Ted was asked to perform at the high school dance, he was one happy _____.
11. When I ran into Mary at the mall, she gave me the cold _____.
12. Stop ____ around! We've got work to do.

Down

1. If you need to learn something quickly, you can take a ____ course.
2. I don't need an exact number right now. A ____ figure is fine.
3. I always prefer cakes and cookies made from ____.
4. If there's one thing teachers hate, it's a___ guy.
5. It's nice when a boss gives you the ____ for your ideas.
9. I have _____ feelings about visiting Puerto Rico in August. On the one hand, it won't be too full of tourists. On the other hand, it will be very hot.
10. Susan is always helping others. She's got a heart of _____.
13. I don't know how I got talked ____ taking a tour of Costa Rica during the rainy season.

ANSWERS TO REVIEW, pp. 160-161

BOB DRIVES A
HARD BARGAIN

Carol from the Village Market calls Bob to discuss Susan's Scrumptious Cookies. Carol and Bob discuss how much Bob will receive for each cookie.

Carol, la del Village Market, llama a Bob para hablar de Susan's Scrumptious Cookies. Carol y Bob discuten cuánto recibirá Bob por cada galleta.

Carol: Hi Bob. **How's it going**?

Bob: Fine thanks, Carol. How are you?

Carol: **Can't complain**. Bob, I've had a chance to **crunch some numbers**. I can pay you 50¢ per cookie.

Bob: That's **out of the question**. At that price, it's not **worth our while**. The ingredients alone cost us 30¢ per cookie.

Carol: Okay, let me **sweeten the deal** — 60¢ per cookie?

Bob: Carol, my wife and I need to **make a living** from this business.

Carol: Okay, okay, you've **twisted my arm**. I'll pay you 75¢ per cookie. **Take it or leave it!**

Bob: **Now you're talking**! We'll take it.

Carol: You **drive a hard bargain**, Bob.

Bob: Yes, but we make a good cookie.

Carol: Let's **get the ball rolling**. Bring me 2,000 cookies on Monday morning by 9 a.m.

IDIOMS – LESSON 11

can't complain – things are going well; I'm fine
no quejarse, todo va bien

EXAMPLE: "How's business, Mike?" — "**Can't complain.** I sold a lot of computers this month."

(to) crunch numbers – to perform calculations (especially financial calculations)
hacer cálculos financieros

EXAMPLE: Sam loves to **crunch numbers,** so he decided to become an accountant.

(to) drive a hard bargain – to be tough in negotiating an agreement; to negotiate something in one's favor
negociar a favor de uno

EXAMPLE: I wanted to pay less for the car, but the salesman **drove a hard bargain.**

(to) get the ball rolling – to get started
empezar

EXAMPLE: Let's **get the ball rolling** on this project. We've only got a week to finish it.

How's it going? – How are you?
¿Qué tal?

EXAMPLE: "**How's it going**?" I asked Ted. "Everything's fine. How are you?" he replied.
SYNONYM: How's life?

(to) make a living – to earn enough money to support oneself
ganarse la vida

EXAMPLE: Many people laugh at him, but Bill actually **makes a living** selling gourmet dog food.

now you're talking – you're saying the right thing; I like what you're saying
¡bien dicho!, ¡así se habla!

EXAMPLE: You want to offer me free tickets to the J. Lo concert? **Now you're talking!**

out of the question – impossible
de ninguna manera

EXAMPLE: My friend Emily wanted me to climb Mount Everest with her, but I told her it was **out of the question**.

(to) sweeten the deal – to make an offer more attractive
hacer el trato más atractivo, dorar la píldora

EXAMPLE: IBM offered to **sweeten the deal** by giving John a company car if he agreed to work for them.

take it or leave it – accept or reject an offer, usually a final one
o lo tomas o lo dejas

EXAMPLE: The highest salary we can offer you is $50,000 a year — **take it or leave it**.

(to) twist (someone's) arm – to persuade someone; to convince someone
convencer

EXAMPLE: Ted didn't want to get another tattoo on his back, but Amber **twisted his arm.**

SYNONYM: Talk (someone) into doing (something). Example: I can't believe I let Alexis **talk me into** driving her to the airport at 6 a.m.

worth one's while – worthy of one's effort or time
valer la pena

EXAMPLE 1: It would be **worth your while** to audition for the game show *Jeopardy*. You'd probably win a lot of money.
EXAMPLE 2: Let me make it **worth your while** to work weekends. I'll pay you an extra $10 per hour on Saturdays and Sundays.

🖎 PRACTICE THE IDIOMS

Abe, owner of Honest Abe's Furniture Store, is talking to Jeff about a new advertising campaign for the store. Jeff owns an advertising agency. Complete the dialogue using these idioms:

get the ball rolling	**drive a hard bargain**
crunch some numbers	**how's it going**
out of the question	**now you're talking**
twisted my arm	**make a living**

Abe: Hi, Jeff. _____?

Jeff: Fine, thanks. I've only scheduled a half hour for this meeting, so we better _____.

Abe: Jeff, I need you to come up with a new advertising campaign for my furniture shop.

Jeff: I've had a chance to ____, and you'll need to pay me $30,000 to come up with some new ideas.

Abe: Thirty thousand dollars? That's really _____!

Jeff: Listen, Abe, I need to _____too. I've got a wife and seven children at home.

Abe: I'll pay you $20,000.

Jeff: If you want quality work, you have to pay for it. Let's say $25,000?

Abe: Okay, okay. You've _____. I'll pay you $23,000.

Jeff: _____. That's a fair price.

Abe: You certainly _____.

Jeff: I know, but you'll be happy with my work.

ANSWERS TO LESSON 11, p. 161

72

BOB'S BIG COOKIE ORDER

The family is gathered around the dinner table. Bob tells them about his deal with the Village Market. He asks his kids for help baking the cookies.

La familia está reunida alrededor de la mesa del comedor. Bob les cuenta su trato con el Village Market. Les pide a sus hijos que le ayuden a hacer las galletas.

Bob: I know I've been **down in the dumps** since I got fired, but **things are looking up** now. The Village Market wants to sell our cookies.

Nicole: That's great news, Dad!

Bob: We're going to have to bake **like crazy** over the weekend. They want 2,000 cookies by Monday.

Nicole: Two thousand cookies in three days? Don't you think you've **bitten off more than you can chew**?

Ted: Yeah, you're going to be **running around like a chicken with its head cut off**!

Susan: Fortunately, there are four of us here. You kids will have to **pitch in** too.

Nicole: Sorry, but I can't. I have to finish Ted's chemistry homework and then I've got to **get going** on my election speech.

Bob: What's that about doing Ted's chemistry homework?

Ted: **Never mind!** Amber will **help out** with the cookies instead of Nicole.

Susan: **For heaven's sake**, Nicole! It's **like pulling teeth** getting you to do any work around here.

IDIOMS – LESSON 12

(to) bite off more than one can chew – to take on more than one is capable of; to take on too much
medir mal sus propias fuerzas

EXAMPLE: Jennifer is having a dinner party for 50 people, and she can't even cook. I think she's **bitten off more than she can chew**.

SYNONYM: *to be* or *to get* in over one's head. Example: Jennifer is **in over her head** with this dinner party!

(to be) down in the dumps – *see Lesson 5*

for heaven's sake! – A way of expressing emotions such as surprise, outrage, or impatience
¡por Dios!

EXAMPLE 1: Hurry up, **for heaven's sake**! You're going to be late for school.

EXAMPLE 2: Oh, **for heaven's sake**! Yesterday, I made three dozen chocolate chip cookies, and today there's only one cookie left!

SYNONYMS: for God's sake, for goodness sake, for Pete's sake

(to) get going – to get started on something
ponerse en marcha

EXAMPLE: If you don't **get going** on your homework soon, you're going to be up all night.

(to) help out – to give assistance
ayudar, echar una mano

EXAMPLE: Amber offered to **help out** in the kitchen by chopping walnuts.

SYNONYM: to lend a hand

like a chicken with its head cut off – in a hysterical manner
como loco, como un histérico

EXAMPLE: When the fire alarm at the hotel started ringing, Doug couldn't find the exit and ran around **like a chicken with its head cut off**.

NOTA: Este modismo se suele usar con el verbo "to run around" como en el ejemplo anterior.

like crazy – with great speed or enthusiasm
rápidamente o con mucho entusiasmo, como loco (lit.)

EXAMPLE 1: When Pete Sampras won the tennis match, the crowd started cheering **like crazy**.
EXAMPLE 2: We worked **like crazy** to finish the project by Friday.

SYNONYM: like mad

like pulling teeth – very difficult
muy difícil

EXAMPLE: It's **like pulling teeth** trying to get Max to talk about his girlfriend.

never mind – don't worry about something; forget it
no importa

EXAMPLE: You forgot to pick up eggs at the supermarket? **Never mind**. I'll get them tomorrow morning.

(to) pitch in – to help
ayudar, echar una mano

EXAMPLE: Nicole offered to **pitch in** and clean up her neighborhood beach. She picked up five plastic cups and an old towel.

SYNONYMS: to lend a hand, to lend a helping hand; to help out

(to) run around – to move about hurriedly
corretear

EXAMPLE: I've been **running around** all day making final arrangements for our trip to Costa Rica tomorrow.

things are looking up – things are improving
la cosa va mejorando

EXAMPLE: Elizabeth found a wonderful new job and just moved into a beautiful new apartment. **Things are really looking up** for her.

✒ PRACTICE THE IDIOMS

Fill in the blank with the missing word:

1) When the sun doesn't shine all winter, it's easy to start feeling down in the _____.

    a) dumps   b) crazy   c) luck

2) Things were so busy at work, I spent the entire week running around like a chicken with its _____ cut off.

    a) beak   b) head   c) neck

3) According to today's newspaper, the economy is improving. Things are looking _____.

    a) up   b) down   c) forward

4) I thought you could help me with my new project. But if you're too busy, never _____. I'll find somebody else.

    a) bother   b) mind   c) worry

5) For heaven's _____! If you don't stop playing those video games, you'll never get your homework done.

    a) angels   b) sake   c) benefit

6) When the school asked Susan to bring cookies to the bake sale, she said she'd be happy to help _____.

    a) in   b) about   c) out

7) When my friend John told me how busy he was preparing for his Halloween party, I offered to pitch _____.

    a) in   b) out   c) him

8) It's like pulling _____ getting Nicole to help out in the kitchen.

    a) hair   b) nails   c) teeth

BONUS PRACTICE

Choose the best substitute for the phrase in bold:

1) Janice is doing all the cooking for her daughter's wedding. I think she's **bitten off more than she can chew**.
   a) accepted too little responsibility
   b) taken too much food into her mouth
   c) taken on more than she can handle

2) If Nicole is going to cover her entire school with election posters, she'd better **get going on** them immediately.
   a) start working on
   b) stop working on
   c) start destroying

3) If you get tired of mowing the lawn, I'd be happy to **help out**.
   a) confuse you
   b) do nothing
   c) assist you

4) Last year, Bill opened a store selling gourmet pet food. This year, he'll open 10 more stores. His business is growing **like crazy!**
   a) very quickly
   b) very slowly
   c) despite being a crazy idea

5) Ever since receiving his rejection letter from Princeton University, Jason has been **down in the dumps**.
   a) happy
   b) sad
   c) encouraged

6) For a long time, Anne couldn't find a boyfriend. But now **things are looking up**. She met a nice guy last weekend.
   a) her love life is getting even worse
   b) her love life is improving
   c) her love life couldn't get much worse

ANSWERS TO LESSON 12, p. 162

Lesson 13

AMBER COMES OVER
TO BAKE COOKIES

Ted's girlfriend Amber comes over to help with the cookies.
Amber has experience baking cookies from a former job.
Susan leaves the kitchen so they can work better.

La novia de Ted, Amber, viene para ayudar con las galletas. Amber
tiene experiencia de otro trabajo que tuvo haciendo galletas. Su-
san se va de la cocina para que puedan trabajar mejor.

Ted: Mom, Amber is here to **lend a hand** with the cookies.

Susan: Hi Amber. Nice to see you again.

Amber: Good to see you too, Mrs. Johnson.

Susan: That's an interesting hairstyle.*

Amber: Thanks. I'm glad you think it's cool. Blue hair is **all the rage** this season.

Susan: Well, I'm going to **take a break** now and let you kids **take over**.

Ted: Don't worry, Mom. Your business is **in good hands** with Amber. She really **knows her stuff**.

Amber: That's true. I used to work at Mrs. Field's Cookies** in the mall.

Susan: You don't work there anymore?

Amber: No, I got fired. I have a real **sweet tooth**, and they told me I was eating too many cookies.

Susan: Well, I'm sure you haven't **lost your touch**.

Amber: I might be a bit **out of practice**.

Ted: Mom, you can watch Amber bake if you want. You might **pick up** a few **tricks of the trade**.

Amber: Yes, **feel free**. As a singer, I'm used to performing before an audience!

Susan: Thanks, but I'm going to **get out of the way**. You know what they say: **too many cooks spoil the broth**!

Amber: Will I see you later tonight?

Susan: Yes, I'll be back in a few hours.

Ted: Mom, why don't you just **call it a night** and go to bed. You've been **working your tail off** all day.

* Cuando alguien dice que algo es "interesante" suele significar que no le gusta, pero quiere ser cortés.

** Mrs. Field's Cookies son galletas gourmet que se venden en centros comerciales estadounidenses.

IDIOMS – LESSON 13

all the rage – the latest fashion
hacer furor, la última moda

EXAMPLE: Have you seen those new alligator-skin cowboy boots? They're **all the rage** this season!

(to) call it a night – to stop an activity for the rest of the night
terminar, irse a casa (por la noche)

EXAMPLE: We spent a few hours walking around downtown Chicago. It was so cold that we were ready to **call it a night** by 9 p.m.

NOTA: También existe la expresión "to call it a day", que quiere decir dejar de trabajar o terminar una actividad al final del día.

feel free – be uninhibited about doing something
Hacer algo sin inhibición, haz lo que quieras, siéntete como en tu casa

EXAMPLE: **Feel free** to take off your shoes.

(to) get out of the way – to move out of the way; to stop interfering with someone's plans or activities
quitarse de en medio

EXAMPLE 1: If you're not planning on helping us prepare dinner, please **get out of the way**. The kitchen is crowded.
EXAMPLE 2: I'll just **get out of the way** and let you plan the party yourself.

(to be) in good hands – in good, competent care
(estar) en buenas manos

EXAMPLE 1: Don't worry – your dog will be **in good hands** while you're on vacation. We'll take her to the New York Dog Spa & Hotel.
EXAMPLE 2: You're **in good hands** with Tony. He's an excellent driver.

NOTA: A menudo verá la expresión "to be in good hands with someone".

(to) know one's stuff – to have an expertise in a field
ser experto, sabérselas todas

EXAMPLE: Steve has been an auto mechanic for 25 years. He really **knows his stuff**.

(to) lend a hand – to help
echar una mano

EXAMPLE: When Amber saw Susan washing the cookie sheets, she offered to **lend a hand**.

(to) lose one's touch – to be no longer able to do something well
ya no poder hacer algo bien, perder el tiento

EXAMPLE: I used to make delicious pies, but this one tastes terrible. I think I've **lost my touch**.

(to be) out of practice – no longer good at doing something
perder la práctica, estar desentrenado

EXAMPLE: Susan used to play the piano all the time, but she hasn't played at all recently. She's really **out of practice**.

(to) pick up – to acquire
aprender

EXAMPLE: Bob **picks up** languages quickly. After just two weeks in Spain, he was already speaking Spanish.
NOTA: "Pick up" tiene otros significados:
1) Recoger. Please **pick up** the newspaper from the floor.
2) Comprar. I'll **pick up** some burritos on my way home.
3) Limpiar. Let's **pick up** the bedroom before the guests arrive.
4) Recoger. Let's **pick up** the pieces of the broken vase before somebody steps on them.
5) Conocer con el fin de conquistar. Jim goes to bars to **pick up** girls.

sweet tooth – an enjoyment of sugary foods
goloso

EXAMPLE: Amber's got a real **sweet tooth**. Last night, she ate a whole box of Godiva chocolates.

(to) take a break – to stop and rest from an activity
tomarse un descanso

EXAMPLE: Bob always worked 10 hours straight, never **taking a break**.

(to) take over – to assume control
hacerse cargo de, asumir

EXAMPLE: After 11 hours of driving, I was getting tired. Fortunately, my friend offered to **take over**.

too many cooks spoil the broth – too many people involved in an activity can ruin it
son muchas manos en un plato

EXAMPLE: After Bob and Susan edited Nicole's college applications, they were worse than when she started. **Too many cooks spoil the broth**.

tricks of the trade – clever shortcuts gained by experience
trucos del oficio, trucos aprendidos por experiencia

EXAMPLE: The new teacher learned some **tricks of the trade** from Mrs. Blackstone, who'd been teaching at the school for 40 years.

(to) work one's tail off – to work very hard
trabajar mucho

EXAMPLE: Jonathan **worked his tail off** to save money for his son's college education.

✎ Practice the Idioms

Fill in the blank with the missing word:

1) When Susan was having trouble lifting her heavy mixer, Bob offered to lend a _____.

   a) finger   b) foot   c) hand

2) Nicole used to play the piano, but she hasn't practiced in five years. She's really _____ practice.

   a) about to   b) into   c) out of

3) You've been working in the kitchen for hours. Why don't you go and _____ a break?

   a) take   b) give   c) do

4) Amber picked up many _____ of the trade while working at Mrs. Field's Cookies in the Stamford Mall.

   a) bits   b) tricks   c) pieces

5) Your shoulder massages are still the best. You haven't ____ your touch.

   a) found   b) lost   c) spoiled

6) After two weeks in Italy, Tom started to pick ___ a few words of Italian, including *cappuccino* and *pizza*.

   a) up   b) out   c) in

7) When Jill got tired of chopping the onions, Jack took _____.

   a) over   b) off   c) away

8) Whenever we need financial advice, we call Suze Orman. She really knows her _____.

   a) things   b) stuff   c) matter

ANSWERS TO LESSON 13, p. 162

AMBER AND TED
HEAT UP THE KITCHEN

Amber and Ted are in the kitchen baking cookies. Amber asks Ted to give her a kiss, but Ted tells her he's too busy. Then he feels guilty and goes to her. But suddenly, they're not alone!

Amber y Ted están en la cocina haciendo galletas. Amber le pide a Ted que le dé un beso, pero Ted le dice que está muy ocupado. Luego se siente culpable y se acerca a ella, pero de pronto ¡no están solos!

Amber: Ted, when I met you it, it was **love at first sight**.

Ted: I was **nuts about** you from the beginning too, Amber. Don't forget, I **broke up with** that girl Tiffany after I met you.

Amber: Come here and give me a kiss.

Ted: **Give me a break**, Amber! We don't have time for that now. We need to **crank out** these cookies.

Amber: You don't really love me, do you?

Ted: Amber, I'm **head over heels in love with you**. But it's **crunch time** with these cookies.

Amber: Cookies, cookies, cookies — you've got a **one-track mind**. ♪ He loves cookies, yeah, yeah, yeah... ♪

Ted: Amber, I need to keep working, but you can **take a break** if you want.

Amber: No, I'll keep **plugging away**...I'm just your cookie slave. **Go ahead, treat me like dirt!**

Ted: Sorry, Amber. Come here and let me give you a quick kiss.

(Susan enters the kitchen)

Susan: Hey, what's going on in here? Are you two making cookies or **making out**?

IDIOMS – LESSON 14

(to) break up with (someone) – to end a relationship with a romantic partner
romper con alguien

EXAMPLE: When Nicole's boyfriend told her he didn't want to see her anymore, she replied, "I can't believe you're **breaking up with** me!"

(to) crank out – to produce rapidly or in a routine manner
producir algo rápidamente o rutinariamente

EXAMPLE: Last night, Nicole **cranked out** 200 signs for her campaign.

crunch time – a short period when there's high pressure to achieve a result
período de tiempo corto en el cual hay mucha presión para conseguir un resultado, al tajo

EXAMPLE: The entire month of December is **crunch time** for Santa Claus.

Give me a break! – stop trying to bother me or fool me
¡déjame en paz!

EXAMPLE: You want me to pay $3 for one cookie? **Give me a break!**

go ahead – to continue; to proceed without hesitation
adelante, sigue

EXAMPLE: We have more than enough food for dinner. **Go ahead** and invite your friend to join us.

NOTA: "Go ahead" también puede usarse como sustantivo, como en la expresión "to give somebody the go ahead", dar permiso para moverse o actuar.

head over heels in love – very much in love
estar perdidamente enamorado

EXAMPLE: During the first years of their marriage, Brad and Jennifer were **head over heels in love** with each other.

love at first sight – an immediate attraction
amor a primera vista

EXAMPLE: It took Allison several months to fall in love with Carl. It wasn't **love at first sight**.

(to) make out – to kiss
besar con mucha pasión

EXAMPLE: Ted and Amber started **making out** at the stoplight and didn't realize that the light had turned green.

NOTA: "Make out" quiere decir besar a alguien apasionadamente, no darle un beso rápido. "Make out" también significa:
  1) Irle. How did you **make out** at the doctor's today?
  2) Divisar o ver con dificultad. It was so foggy, I could barely **make out** the street signs.
  3) Rellenar un formulario escrito. Please **make out** a check for $14.95.

(to be) nuts about – like very much
gustarle mucho, loco por

EXAMPLE: Ted has every single Rolling Stones album — he's **nuts about** that band.
SYNONYM: crazy about. Example: Ted's really **crazy about** the Rolling Stones.

(to have a) one-track mind – having all thoughts directed to just one thing or activity
de un solo interés, pensar sólo en una cosa

EXAMPLE: Rob thinks about girls all the time. He's got a **one-track mind**.

(to) plug away (at something) – to proceed with a boring or routine task
proceder con una tarea aburrida o rutinaria

EXAMPLE: Only 842 more cookies to bake. Let's keep **plugging away**!

take a break – *Vea el capítulo 13*

(to) treat (someone) like dirt – to behave in a nasty way towards someone; to treat someone poorly
tratar mal a alguien

EXAMPLE: Nobody was surprised when Nicole's boyfriend broke up with her, since she **treated him like dirt**.

✎ PRACTICE THE IDIOMS

Susan is telling the story of how she met her husband. Fill in the blanks, using the following idioms:

love at first sight	**go ahead**
plugging away	**treated him like dirt**
crunch time	**crank out**
making out	**crazy about**
broke up with	**head over heels in love**

I met Bob in college. He was in my English Literature class. I liked him right away. For me, it was _____. I wrote him several love poems, though I never gave them to him. Then I found out that he had a girlfriend. I saw him

_____ with a girl named Joyce. It looked like she was _____ Bob too. But later that week, I heard that she was a nasty person and that she _____.

So I decided to _____ and ask him to the movies. He said he was too busy. It was _____, and he had to _____ a paper for literature class and study for several exams. But I didn't give up. I kept _____. Then one day he _____ Joyce and asked me out to dinner. That was 25 years ago, and we're still together. Fortunately, we're still _____ with each other!

ANSWERS TO LESSON 14, p. 162

"Remember the rule of thumb –
imagine your audience naked."

NICOLE PRACTICES HER ELECTION SPEECH

Nicole is running for student body president. She must give a speech next week. She discusses the speech with her mother.

Nicole se ha presentado a las elecciones para presidente del alumnado. Tiene que dar un discurso la semana siguiente. Habla de su discurso con su madre.

Susan: **What's up**, Nicole?

Nicole: I **pulled an all-nighter** working on my election speech.

Susan: **No wonder** you **look like** a **basket case**! Did you finish your speech?

Nicole: Yes, at 6 a.m.

Susan: That must be a **load off your mind**!

Nicole: It's not. I've got to give the speech tomorrow in front of 1,500 people. I'm a **nervous wreck**!

Susan: Just remember the old **rule of thumb**: Imagine your audience naked.

Nicole: That's gross! Why would I want to do that?

Susan: According to **conventional wisdom**, it'll make you less nervous.

Nicole: Only practice will **do the trick**.

Susan: Okay, let's hear the speech.

Nicole: Good afternoon, everyone. There are four candidates running for president. You think you have several choices. **In reality**, you have just one choice: me!

Susan: You can't say that. You'll **turn off** your audience immediately.

Nicole: It sounds like I have a **big head**?

Susan: **I'll say!**

IDIOMS – LESSON 15

basket case [slang] – someone in a useless or hopeless condition
loco, en condición inútil o desesperada

EXAMPLE: After working a 12-hour day and then coming home and cooking dinner for her family, Samantha felt like a **basket case**.

(to have a) big head – arrogant; too proud of oneself
arrogante

EXAMPLE: Stop bragging so much about the award you got at work! People will think you've got a **big head**.

SYNONYM: to be full of oneself. Example: Jessica is really **full of herself**. She's always talking about how smart she is.

conventional wisdom – a widely held belief
creencia popular

EXAMPLE: According to **conventional wisdom**, a diet high in salt can cause high blood pressure.

(to) do the trick – to achieve the desired results
conseguir los resultados deseados

EXAMPLE: Juan changed the light bulb and said, "That should **do the trick!**"

I'll say! – yes, definitely!
¡Desde luego!

EXAMPLE: "Did you enjoy the Madonna concert?" — "**I'll say!**"

in reality – in fact; actually
en realidad

EXAMPLE: Ted thinks it'll be easy to become a rock star. **In reality**, it will take years of hard work.

load off one's mind – a relief
quitarse un peso de encima

EXAMPLE: When Amber called Ted to tell him that she arrived home safely, it was a big **load off his mind**.

look like – have the appearance of
parecer

EXAMPLE: Before agreeing to go out on a date with her, Carl wanted to know what my cousin Maria **looked like**.

NOTA: La expresión "it looks like" significa "parece probable que..." It's snowing, so **it looks like** the schools will be closed today.

nervous wreck – a person feeling very worried
nervioso, preocupado

EXAMPLE: Whenever Nicole rode on the back of her friend's motorcycle, Susan was a **nervous wreck**.

no wonder – it's not surprising
ya lo decía yo

EXAMPLE: **No wonder** you're cold — it's January and you're walking around outside without a coat!

(to) pull an all-nighter – to stay up all night to do work
estudiar (o trabajar) toda la noche

EXAMPLE: Ted **pulled an all-nighter** to study for his chemistry test and ended up falling asleep in class the next day.

rule of thumb – a useful principle
por lo general

EXAMPLE: When cooking fish, a good **rule of thumb** is 10 minutes in the oven for each inch of thickness.

(to) turn off – to cause to feel dislike or revulsion
disgustar

EXAMPLE 1: I used to be friends with Monica, but she gossiped all the time and it really **turned me off**.
EXAMPLE 2: After his bad experience with chemistry class, Ted will probably be **turned off** to the subject forever.

NOTA: La expresión también significa "apagar". **Turn off** the lights when you leave the room.

what's up? – *Vea el capítulo 10*

✍ PRACTICE THE IDIOMS

Choose the best substitute for the phrase in bold:

1) Ted didn't start studying for his chemistry test until the night before. Then he had to **pull an all-nighter**.
   a) get plenty of rest before an exam
   b) stay up all night studying
   c) sleep late

2) After working on it for months, I finally gave my presentation this morning. That was certainly **a load off my mind**!
   a) a relief
   b) difficult
   c) easy

3) Nicole was **turned off** when Todd, her date, started picking his teeth with a toothpick during dinner.
   a) left the room
   b) became interested
   c) lost all interest

94

4) According to **conventional wisdom**, you shouldn't ask about salary on your first interview.
   a) accepted beliefs
   b) outdated beliefs
   c) smart people

5) Ted had to perform his music before one of the most important talent agents in the country. It's not surprising that he was **a nervous wreck**.
   a) confident
   b) very worried
   c) exhausted

6) Girls cheered and blew kisses whenever Ted performed his music. Amber worried that he'd **get a big head**.
   a) get a headache
   b) become arrogant
   c) find a new girlfriend

7) People keep telling Fred that he looks **like a basket case**. Maybe it's because he hasn't slept in weeks.
   a) really great
   b) angry
   c) terrible

8) Do you have a headache? Here, take two aspirin. That should **do the trick**.
   a) make you feel better
   b) perform magic
   c) make you feel worse

ANSWERS TO LESSON 15, p. 162

Review for Lessons 11-15

Choose the best substitute for the phrase or sentence in bold:

1) Nicole didn't want to go to the party, but her friend **twisted her arm**.
   a) persuaded her
   b) hurt her arm
   c) agreed with her

2) Amber needs to go on a diet and lose 10 pounds, but it's difficult for her because **she has such a sweet tooth**.
   a) she has a loose tooth
   b) she has emotional problems
   c) she likes to eat sweets

3) Amber likes to design handbags as a hobby, but she's not sure she could **make a living at it**.
   a) do it for the rest of her life
   b) earn enough money to support herself
   c) do it all day long

4) Ted wanted to travel to Miami for a rock concert. His mother told him it was **out of the question**.
   a) a good idea
   b) still a possibility
   c) not a possibility

5) Nicole **worked her tail off,** making hundreds of posters for her campaign.
   a) worked very hard
   b) worked until her tail fell off
   c) made her friends work hard

6) **It's crunch time**. Ted has to write six papers in two days.
   a) It's a very busy time.
   b) It's a time to relax.
   c) It's a period of time filled with fun and laughter.

7) My 95-year old neighbor was cutting her grass on a hot summer day. I offered to **lend a hand**.
   a) give her my hand
   b) help her
   c) drive her to the hospital

8) Jennifer **treats her husband like dirt**. I don't know why he doesn't just leave her.
   a) is very nice to her husband
   b) asks her husband to do the gardening
   c) is nasty to her husband

9) Tattoos are **all the rage**. Many kids are getting them.
   a) something that makes you angry
   b) very popular
   c) easy to get

10) **Things are looking up for Bob**. He's already found a new job working for his wife.
    a) Bob's situation is getting worse.
    b) Bob's situation is improving.
    c) Bob always focuses on positive things.

11) Susan volunteered to host 45 exchange students from China. Now she fears she's **bitten off more than she can chew**.
    a) accepted an easy assignment
    b) taken on a bigger task than she can handle
    c) ordered too much Chinese food

12) If Ted doesn't **get going on** his chemistry homework soon, he's going to be up all night.
    a) start doing
    b) stop doing
    c) leave the house with

CROSSWORD PUZZLE

Across

2. My old job was boring. All I did was _____ numbers all day.
4. Bob went to visit the Village Market to get the ___ rolling on the cookie business.
5. You didn't take out the garbage yet? Never___! I'll do it myself.
7. Donna ate the whole apple pie herself. I guess she has a _____ tooth.
9. Jim never thought he could sell designer watches on street corners, but his brother taught him the _____ of the trade.
11. You've been working at the computer for hours. Why don't you take a _____?
12. After her boyfriend broke up with her, Anne was feeling down in the _____.
13. Mini-skirts were all the _____ last summer.

Down

1. Liz used to sing opera, but she hasn't performed in years. She's out of _____.
3. Bill thinks he's the smartest guy in the world. His friends think he just has a big _____.
6. I don't like horror movies, but John _____ my arm and I agreed to see "Murder on Main Street."
8. My car wasn't running well so I changed the oil. That should do the _____.
10. After the car accident, Betty was a _____ wreck whenever she drove.
11. When I don't get eight hours of sleep, I feel like a ___ case in the morning.

ANSWERS TO REVIEW, p. 163

BOB BRINGS THE COOKIES TO THE VILLAGE MARKET

Bob brings Carol the cookies. He tells Carol that baking the cookies was easy because he had lots of help.

Bob le trae las galletas a Carol. Le dice a Carol que fue fácil hacer las galletas porque tuvo mucha ayuda.

Carol: Bob, how did the baking go?

Bob: Slow **at first**, but we're **getting the hang of it**.

Carol: Once you **learn the ropes**, it becomes **second nature**.

Bob: **To tell you the truth**, I thought that baking 2,000 cookies would be a **pain in the neck**. But we managed to **round up** some helpers, and it was a **piece of cake**.

Carol: Well, thanks for coming **in person** with the cookies.

Bob: No problem. When will you need more?

Carol: It depends on how many we sell today.

Bob: How many do you think you'll sell?

Carol: Maybe 500, maybe 2,000. **Your guess is as good as mine. In any case**, I'll **keep you posted**.

Bob: Okay. Just **give me a ring** as soon as you know.

IDIOMS – LESSON 16

at first – in the beginning
al principio

EXAMPLE: Nicole didn't like *Don Quixote* **at first**, but after 200 pages she started to get into it.

(to) get the hang of (something) – to learn how to do something; to acquire an effective technique
aprender a hacer algo

EXAMPLE: Billy had trouble learning how to ride a bike, but after a few months he finally **got the hang of it.**

(to) give (someone) a ring – to telephone someone
llamar a alguien por teléfono

EXAMPLE: **Give me a ring** tomorrow so we can discuss plans for this weekend.

SYNONYM: to give someone a buzz [slang]

in any case – whatever the fact is; certainly
en cualquier caso, ciertamente

EXAMPLE: We can either go to the new Star Wars movie or see a play tonight. **In any case**, you'll need to be at my house by six o'clock.

SYNONYM: in any event

in person – personally; in one's physical presence
en persona

EXAMPLE: Tim hoped that he and Amanda would get along as well **in person** as they did over the Internet.

(to) keep posted – to provide up-to-date information
mantener informado

EXAMPLE: **Keep me posted** about your plans for the summer. If you're going to be at your cottage on the lake, I'd love to come visit.

SYNONYM: to keep someone in the loop. Example: **Keep me in the loop** regarding your summer plans.

(to) learn the ropes – to learn the basics
aprender lo básico

EXAMPLE: Mark **learned the ropes** of the restaurant business by working as a cook at the Outback Steakhouse.

pain in the neck – an annoyance
un pesado, una molestia

EXAMPLE: Yesterday I had to stay home all day and wait for the repairman. What a **pain in the neck**!

SYNONYMS: pain in the ass [grosero]; pain in the butt [grosero]

piece of cake – very easy
muy fácil

EXAMPLE: Nicole finished her physics exam in just 25 minutes. It was a **piece of cake**.

SYNONYM: easy as pie

(to) round up – to gather people together
reunir (a la gente)

EXAMPLE: The town **rounded up** 200 volunteers to search for the hiker, who was lost in the woods of Yosemite National Park.

second nature – a behavior that has been practiced for so long, it seems to have been there always
algo que se ha practicado tanto, que parece que siempre se ha sabido hacer

EXAMPLE: Laura has been arguing with her husband every day for the past 20 years, so by now it's just **second nature**.

to tell you the truth – to speak openly
a decir verdad

EXAMPLE 1: **To tell you the truth,** Ted isn't a very good student.

EXAMPLE 2: **To tell you the truth,** Susan's cookies aren't that delicious.

your guess is as good as mine – I don't know any more than you do
usted sabe tanto como yo

EXAMPLE: Will we ever find intelligent life on other planets? **Your guess is as good as mine.**

✎ PRACTICE THE IDIOMS

Fill in the blank with the appropriate word:

1) When Nicole drove her car for the first time, she was really nervous. Now, after an entire year, it's _____ nature.

    a) first   b) second   c) third

2) I can't believe I won. To _____ you the truth, I never thought I'd be able to beat you at tennis.

    a) say   b) tell   c) explain

3) Nicole was going to mail her college application to Yale. But then she decided to go to New Haven and deliver it ___ person.

    a) on   b) at   c) in

4) After a snowstorm, it can be a real pain in the _____ driving to work in the morning.

    a) head   b) arm   c) neck

5) The meeting in Dallas was cancelled, but, in ____ case, we still need to go there.

    a) all   b) any   c) about

6) Starting a new job is difficult in the beginning. It gets easier once you learn the ____.

    a) ropes   b) chains   c) ties

7) Bob and Susan thought getting rich would be very difficult. But thanks to their cookie business, it was a piece of _____.

    a) cookie   b) cake   c) pie

8) Let's go to the movies tonight. I'll look in the newspaper and ___ you a ring after I see what's playing.

    a) offer   b) take   c) give

ANSWERS TO LESSON 16, p. 163

CAROL TELLS BOB THE GOOD NEWS

Carol phones Bob to tell him the cookies are selling very well and that she needs another 1,000 by the morning. Bob isn't sure he can make the cookies so quickly, but Carol insists.

Carol llama a Bob por teléfono para decirle que las galletas se están vendiendo muy bien y que necesita otras 1.000 para la mañana siguiente. Bob no está seguro de poder hacer las galletas tan rápido, pero Carol insiste.

Carol: Bob, your wife's cookies are **selling like hotcakes**!

Bob: How many did you sell, Carol?

Carol: We've **sold out**. I need more **right away**! Bring me another 1,000 by tomorrow at 9 a.m.

Bob: That's a **tall order**, Carol.

Carol: Don't **blow it**, Bob! Susan's Scrumptious Cookies could really **take off**.

Bob: I know, but I'm not sure we have enough time to bake all those cookies.

Carol: Bake all night if you have to. **Burn the midnight oil**! If you work hard now, you'll be **sitting pretty** in a few years.

Bob: **Rest assured** that I'll **do my best** to **deliver the goods**.

Carol: Okay, now let's stop the **chitchat.**You've got work to do!

IDIOMS – LESSON 17

(to) blow it – to spoil an opportunity
perder una oportunidad

EXAMPLE: The actress got nervous and forgot all of her lines. She really **blew it!**

(to) burn the midnight oil – to stay up late studying or working
trabajar o estudiar toda la noche

EXAMPLE: Ted **burned the midnight oil** studying for his chemistry test.

chitchat – casual conversation; gossip
cháchara, parloteo, chismeo

EXAMPLE: Greg told Mary to stop the **chitchat** and get back to work.

NOTA: Chitchat también puede ser un verbo. Amber and Ted were **chitchatting** all night long.

(to) deliver the goods – to meet expectations; to do what's required
cumplir expectativas

EXAMPLE: Peter thought Bob wasn't **delivering the goods**, so he fired him.

SYNONYM: to cut the mustard. Example: If you can't **cut the mustard** here, you'll have to find a new job.

(to) do one's best – to try as hard as possible
hacer lo posible

EXAMPLE: Although Ted **did his best**, he still failed his chemistry test.

SYNONYMS: to do one's damnedest; to give it one's all

rest assured – be sure

no te preocupes

EXAMPLE: **Rest assured** that the police will find the thieves.

right away – immediately

ahora mismo

EXAMPLE: When Meg realized her house was on fire, she called the fire department **right away**.

(to) sell like hotcakes – to sell fast; to be a popular item

venderse rápidamente, venderse como un pan bendito

EXAMPLE: Those new Fubu blue jeans are **selling like hotcakes**. All the girls love them.

(to be) sitting pretty – in a good position (often financially)

en buena posición (financieramente)

EXAMPLE: After Chad won the lottery, he was really **sitting pretty**. He quit his job and bought a mansion in Malibu, California.

sold out – completely sold

agotado

EXAMPLE: Tiffany was really disappointed when she found out that the Britney Spears concert was **sold out**.

(to) take off – to become popular; to grow suddenly

popularizarse rápidamente

EXAMPLE 1: Julia Roberts' career really **took off** with the film "Pretty Woman."

EXAMPLE 2: Sales at stores always **take off** around the holidays.

NOTA: "Take off" tiene otros significados:
1. Quitarse. Please **take off** your shoes before coming inside our apartment. We just vacuumed this morning.
2. Irse. We're **taking off** now. See you later!
3. Deducir. The waiter forgot to bring us drinks, so he **took $10 off** the bill.

tall order – a task or goal that is difficult to achieve

mucho pedir

EXAMPLE: It'll be a **tall order** to find a new governor as popular as the current one.

Choose the most appropriate reply to the following statements:

1) "Bob, your cookies are delicious. They're selling like hotcakes."

    Bob's reply:
    a) "I'm not surprised. My family has always loved them."
    b) "What? I thought people would buy more."
    c) "Yes, they are best when served hot."

2) "Bob, I know you can get me 1,000 cookies by morning. Don't blow it!"

    Bob's reply:
    a) "I never blow on the cookies. I let them cool down by themselves."
    b) "Don't worry. I'll be sure to get you the cookies by 9 a.m."
    c) "Thanks. I'll take my time then."

3) "Bob, I've got some great news for you. All of your chocolate chip cookies have sold out!"

    Bob's reply:
    a) "Great. I'd better make more."
    b) "I guess people don't like them."
    c) "How many are left?"

4) "Ted, if you and Amber don't stop the chitchat, you'll never finish your homework."

    Ted's reply:
    a) "Okay, we'll stay up all night talking."
    b) "Okay, we'll stop talking and start hitting the books."
    c) "Yes, Amber is helping a lot with my homework."

5) "Ted, ask Amber to come over right away to help bake cookies."

Ted's reply:
a) "Okay. I'll tell her to come over next Saturday."
b) "Okay. I'll tell her to come over immediately."
c) "Okay. I'll ask her to go away."

6) "Bob, if you work hard now, you'll be sitting pretty in a couple of years."

Bob's reply:
a) "Thank you. I am looking forward to feeling pretty."
b) "I don't enjoy sitting for long periods of time."
c) "Great. I'd love to be able to stop working and start relaxing more."

7) "Nicole, getting elected to the United States Senate is a very tall order."

Nicole's reply:
a) "I know, but I love a good challenge."
b) "I agree. It should be very easy."
c) "I know. I've already put in my order."

8) "Bob, I suggest you burn the midnight oil and make 1,000 cookies tonight."

Bob's reply:
a) "Okay. I'll go to sleep at midnight and wake up at 10 a.m."
b) "Yes, we'll need quite a bit of oil for the cookies."
c) "Okay. I'll work all night and finish up by morning."

ANSWERS TO LESSON 17, p. 163

Lesson 18

EVERYONE BAKES COOKIES

*Bob tells his family the cookies are selling well. He asks his
kids to help bake more cookies for tomorrow. Nicole says she's
too busy to lend a hand.*

*Bob le dice a su familia que las galletas se están vendiendo
bien. Les pide a sus hijos que le ayuden a hacer más galletas
para mañana. Nicole dice que está demasiado ocupada para
echarle una mano.*

Bob: The cookies are **selling like hotcakes**!

Ted: **Way to go**, Dad!

Bob: I need you kids to **help out** tonight with the cookies.
We need another thousand by morning.

Nicole: One thousand by tomorrow morning? That's impossible!

Ted: Amber and I will **lend a hand**. She's a real **night owl**,
so she won't mind **staying up** late.

Bob: Nicole, we'll need your help too.

Nicole: Bake cookies the night before the elections? **Nothing
doing**!

Ted: **Lighten up**, **big shot**! You're running for high school
president, not President of the United States.

Nicole: Ted, you really **get on my nerves** sometimes.

Bob: Okay, kids, let's stop **fooling around**. We need to **get the show on the road!**

IDIOMS – LESSON 18

big shot – a powerful or important person
persona importante o poderosa, pez gordo

EXAMPLE: Martin has become a real **big shot** in Hollywood.

(to) fool around – to waste time, or spend it in a silly way
perder el tiempo

EXAMPLE: If we keep **fooling around** here, we'll never finish making lunch!

NOTA: Esta expresión también puede significar "tener relaciones sexuales casuales". Example: Steve and Tanya were **fooling around** in the back seat of the car when the policeman knocked on the window.

(to) get on one's nerves – to annoy or irritate someone
crisparle los nervios, irritar a alguien

EXAMPLE: The dog next door barks all night. It really **gets on my nerves**.
SYNONYMS: to get under someone's skin; to bug someone [slang]

(to) get the show on the road – to start working; to begin an undertaking
empezar a trabajar

EXAMPLE: We can't afford to waste any more time — let's **get the show on the road!**
SYNONYMS: to get a move on; to get going

(to) help out – *Vea el capítulo 12*

(to) lend a hand – *Vea el capítulo 13*

(to) lighten up – to stop taking things so seriously
no tomárselo tan en serio

EXAMPLE: "**Lighten up!** I'm sure Ted was only joking when he said your guitar playing gave him a headache."
SYNONYMS: chill out [slang]; take it easy

night owl – a person who enjoys being active late at night
persona a la que le gusta estar activa por la noche, ave nocturna

EXAMPLE: Sara goes to sleep every night at 3 a.m. She's a real **night owl**.

Nothing doing! – Not a chance!
¡Ni hablar!

EXAMPLE: "You want me to buy this bridge from you for a million bucks? **Nothing doing!**"
SYNONYMS: No way! Not on your life!

(to) sell like hotcakes – *Vea el capítulo 17*

(to) stay up – not to go to bed; to stay awake
no acostarse

EXAMPLE: Ted and Amber **stayed up** all night talking about the meaning of life.

Way to go! – *Vea el capítulo 4*

✑ PRACTICE THE IDIOMS

Fill in the blank with the appropriate word:

1) I was really proud of my friend for winning an Olympic medal. "Way to ____!" I told her.

    a) do   b) succeed   c) go

2) Amber loves to cook, so she never minds lending ____ in the kitchen.

    a) herself   b) a hand   c) her hands

3) Vanessa is definitely not a night ____. She likes to be in bed by 9 o'clock every night.

    a) bird   b) hawk   c) owl

4) After Mr. Trimble was elected president of the company, he thought he was a real ____ shot.

    a) big   b) huge   c) large

5) You're taking everything too seriously. You need to lighten ___.

    a) above   b) up   c) down

6) Let's go! We're already late. Let's get the show on the _____.

    a) street   b) way   c) road

7) When people near me whisper during a movie, it really ___ on my nerves.

    a) gets   b) acts   c) scratches

8) Nicole's teacher asked her to help a new exchange student from Argentina with her English homework. Nicole was happy to help _____.

    a) around   b) out   c) in

BONUS PRACTICE

Choose the best substitute for the phrase or sentence in bold:

1) You want me to drive you all the way to Toronto during this snowstorm? **Nothing doing!**
    a) Great idea!
    b) No problem!
    c) Not a chance!

2) Len and Ben, college roommates, **stayed up** until 3 a.m. talking and drinking beer. No wonder they didn't wake up until noon the next day!
    a) didn't go to bed
    b) went to bed
    c) didn't eat dinner

3) Michael used to work the late shift at McDonald's — from midnight to 8 a.m. He didn't mind since he's **a night owl**.
   a) a wise person
   b) a person who goes to sleep early
   c) a person who likes to stay up late

4) The man behind me on the bus wouldn't stop whistling. It really **got on my nerves**!
   a) entertained me
   b) annoyed me
   c) relaxed me

5) Our plane leaves in just two hours. If we don't **get the show on the road**, we're going to miss it.
   a) go into the street
   b) get ready to go
   c) call the airline

6) You want to attend Yale University? Call my friend Penny. She's **a real big shot** on the admissions committee.
   a) a powerful person
   b) a big mouth
   c) a useless person

7) Ted was **fooling around** with his friends when he should've been studying for his chemistry test.
   a) acting like a fool
   b) putting time to good use
   c) wasting time

8) You got a big promotion at work? **Way to go!**
   a) Too bad!
   b) Good job!
   c) Sorry to hear that!

ANSWERS TO LESSON 18, p. 164

NICOLE'S CLOSE ELECTION

Nicole loses the election at school. She doesn't want to accept it, so she looks for excuses. Ted encourages her to accept defeat and move on.

Nicole pierde las elecciones en el colegio. No quiere aceptarlo, así que busca excusas. Ted la anima a aceptar la derrota y seguir adelante.

Nicole: I lost the election **by a hair** — just 10 votes! But I'm not **giving up**.

Ted: **Give me a break**, Nicole. You lost. **Live with it**!

Nicole: But I was a **sure thing**! If I hadn't stayed up so late baking cookies, I wouldn't have **messed up** my speech.

Ted: **Get real**, Nicole.

Nicole: It's your fault, Ted. I lost because your friends didn't vote for me!

Ted: Don't try to **put the blame on** me! **I gave it my best shot**.

Nicole: They must've made a mistake while counting the votes. I'll demand a re-count on Monday and **set the record straight**.

Ted: Don't **make a fool of yourself**, Nicole. **Face it**, Andrea won the election **fair and square**!

Nicole: Well, I just don't know where I **went wrong**.

Susan: Here, take a chocolate chip cookie. That'll **cheer you up for sure!**

IDIOMS – LESSON 19

by a hair – very narrowly
por poco, por los pelos

EXAMPLE: Larry won the bicycle race **by a hair**. The second-place winner came in just a second behind him.

(to) cheer up – *Vea el capítulo 6*

Face it – *Vea el capítulo 1*

fair and square – honestly
con absoluta honradez

EXAMPLE: Did George Bush win the 2000 presidential election **fair and square**? That depends on whether you ask a Democrat or a Republican!

for sure – definitely
seguramente

EXAMPLE: This year, Tom Cruise will win an Academy Award **for sure**.

Get real – *Vea el capítulo 3*

(to) give it one's best shot – to try as hard as one can
hacer lo posible

EXAMPLE: Jennifer lost the tennis match, but at least she **gave it her best shot**.
SYNONYM: to give it the old college try

give me a break – *Vea el capítulo 14*

(to) give up – to admit defeat; to surrender
rendirse

EXAMPLE: Bill **gave up** golf after realizing he'd never be good at it.
SYNONYM: to throw in the towel

(to) go wrong – to make a mistake; to go astray
salir mal

EXAMPLE: Follow the directions I gave you, and you can't **go wrong**.

(to) live with it – to accept a difficult reality
aceptar una realidad difícil

EXAMPLE: Your boss is an idiot. **Live with it**.
SYNONYMS: to deal with it; to come to terms with it
NOTA: También existe la expresión "learn to live with it", que significa "acostumbrarse a algo desagradable o molesto". Nancy knew Joe would always throw his dirty clothes on the floor. She'd just have to **learn to live with it**.

(to) make a fool of oneself – to cause oneself to look stupid
hacer el ridículo

EXAMPLE: Dan drank too much at the party and then **made a fool of** himself.

(to) mess up – to make a mistake; to spoil an opportunity
cometer un error, perder una oportunidad

EXAMPLE: Amber **messed up** and put salt instead of sugar in the cookies.
SYNONYM: screw up [slang]
NOTA: "Mess up" también significa "desordenar". Whenever Jackie leaves her house, her dog Kelly goes into her bedroom and **messes up** her bed.

(to) put the blame on (someone) – to name somebody else as responsible for a misdeed or misfortune
echarle la culpa a alguien

EXAMPLE: Mrs. Lopez **put the blame on** her husband for losing their life savings in the stock market.
SYNONYM: to pass the buck

(to) set the record straight – to correct an inaccurate account
aclarar las cosas

EXAMPLE: Ken knew his father was innocent, and he hoped he could **set the record straight** one day.

sure thing – an outcome that is assured
seguro

EXAMPLE: Gary bet all his money on a horse named Trixie, thinking she was a **sure thing**.

117

✒ PRACTICE THE IDIOMS

Ted is angry at Nicole because she didn't do a good job on his chemistry homework. Fill in the blanks using the following idioms:

give me a break	**cheer you up**
sure thing	**for sure**
put the blame on me	**live with it**
give it my best shot	**messed up**

Ted: Nicole, my teacher gave me back my chemistry homework. I got a terrible grade! I thought _____ you'd help me get an A+.

Nicole: I'm sorry. I really did _____, but I guess it wasn't good enough.

Ted: Not good enough? That's right. You really _____!

Nicole: You never should've asked me to do your homework. Don't try to _____ for your bad grades.

Ted: Yes, my mistake. I thought you were a _____!

Nicole: So you'll get a bad grade in chemistry. Just learn to _____. Here, take one of Mom's fresh-baked cookies. It'll help _____.

Ted: You think a stupid cookie will cheer me up? _____!

ANSWERS TO LESSON 19, p. 164

BOB GETS AN ANGRY CALL FROM CAROL

Carol calls Bob to tell him that a customer found a hair in her cookie. Bob wants Carol to forget about this, but Carol thinks it's very serious. She refuses to buy any more cookies from Bob.

Carol llama a Bob para decirle que una cliente encontró un pelo en su galleta. Bob quiere que Carol se olvide de esto, pero Carol cree que es algo muy serio. Se niega a comprarle más galletas a Bob.

Carol: Bob, a lady came into the Village Market today **ranting and raving**.

Bob: Oh yeah? What happened?

Carol: She found a blue hair in her chocolate chip cookie!

Bob: Aha. I can see how she'd be **taken aback.**

Carol: Does anybody in your family have blue hair?

Bob: **As a matter of fact**, my son's girlfriend Amber has blue hair.

Carol: Bob, I can't sell your cookies anymore.

Bob: Aren't you **blowing things out of proportion**?

Carol: The health department would **throw the book at me** if they **found out** about this.

Bob: Couldn't we just **sweep this under the rug?**

Carol: No. This is too serious.

Bob: But I was just **getting a handle on** the cookie business. Now what will I do? I don't have any other way of **making a living**!

Carol: **My heart goes out to you,** Bob, but you need to **get your act together**. I want to sell *chocolate chip* cookies, not *hair* cookies!

Bob: I guess I just **knocked myself out** for the past week for nothing.

Carol: Clearly!

IDIOMS – LESSON 20

as a matter of fact – in fact; actually
de hecho

EXAMPLE: We need more milk? **As a matter of fact**, I was just going to ask you to go shopping.

(to) blow things out of proportion – to exaggerate
exagerar

EXAMPLE: They sent a 12 year-old boy to jail for biting his babysitter? Don't you think they're **blowing things out of proportion**?

SYNONYM: to make a mountain out of a molehill

(to) find out – to learn; to discover
averiguar, descubrir

EXAMPLE: Maria is calling the theater to **find out** what time the movie starts.

(to) get a handle on – to gain an understanding of
llegar a entender

EXAMPLE: This new computer program is very difficult. I still haven't **gotten a handle on** it.
SYNONYM: to get a grasp of

(to) get one's act together – to get organized; to start operating more effectively
organizarse

EXAMPLE: If Ted **gets his act together** now, he might be able to get into a good college.
SYNONYM: to clean up one's act. Example: If Ted wants to attend New York University, he'd better **clean up his act**.

(to) knock oneself out – to work very hard at something (sometimes too hard)
trabajar mucho (a veces demasiado)

EXAMPLE: Ted **knocked himself out** getting votes for Nicole, and she didn't even say thank you.

NOTA: Esta expresión se suele usar de forma negativa. "Don't knock yourself out!" significa "No te esfuerces, no vale la pena". **Don't knock yourself out** for Lisa — she won't appreciate it anyway!

(to) make a living – *Vea el capítulo 11*

one's heart goes out to (someone) – feel sorry for someone
compadecer

EXAMPLE: **My heart goes out to** all the people who lost their homes in the earthquake.

(to) rant and rave – to talk loudly, often in anger
despotricar

EXAMPLE: A customer in the video rental store was **ranting and raving** that the DVD he rented was broken.

(to) sweep (something) under the rug – to hide something, often a scandal
ocultar, a menudo un escándalo

EXAMPLE: "Senator, don't try to **sweep it under the rug**. Everybody knows about your affair with the intern."

taken aback – surprised
tomarle por sorpresa

EXAMPLE: Nicole was **taken aback** when her friend Rosa told her she no longer wanted to hang out with her.

(to) throw the book at someone – to punish or chide severely
castigar con todo rigor

EXAMPLE: When Ted failed his chemistry test the second time, his teacher really **threw the book** at him.

✑ PRACTICE THE IDIOMS

Choose the best substitute for the phrase in bold:

1) After Nicole lost the election, she started **ranting and raving**.
   a) complaining loudly
   b) speaking quietly
   c) asking many questions

2) When a stranger approached me on the bus and asked to borrow my cell phone, I was **taken aback**.
   a) disappointed
   b) surprised
   c) delighted

3) When George showed up for work five minutes late, his boss Beth threatened to fire him. Beth is known for **blowing things out of proportion**.
   a) making a big deal out of a small things
   b) lying
   c) creating extra work for someone

4) My apartment is always messy. I need to **get my act together** and start cleaning it once a week.
   a) start pretending
   b) gather a group of people together
   c) get organized

5) **My heart goes out to** all the homeless people lying outside my apartment building in February.
   a) I help
   b) I feel sorry for
   c) I feel good about

6) I just **found out** yesterday that Amber never washes her hands before making cookies. Ted told me.
   a) saw
   b) overheard
   c) learned

7) Ted has three parking tickets that he still hasn't paid. He's afraid one day the police will **throw the book at him**.
   a) give him another ticket
   b) arrest him
   c) read to him

8) Ted's chemistry homework was much more difficult than Nicole had expected. She just couldn't seem to **get a handle on it**.
   a) finish it
   b) understand it
   c) hold it in her hands

ANSWERS TO LESSON 20, p. 164

Review for Lessons 16-20

Fill in the blank with the appropriate word:

1) My aunt and uncle are really sitting _____. They made a lot of money in the stock market.

   a) rich   b) poor   c) pretty

2) Lighten _____! You need to stop taking your job so seriously.

    a) it   b) up   c) over

3) After a week, my houseguests really started to get ____ my nerves. They made long-distance phone calls to Santiago, drank all my wine, and slept until noon every day.

    a) by   b) in   c) on

4) Amber likes to stay up past midnight every night. She's what you'd call a _____ owl.

    a) night   b) busy   c) day

5) Mildred thought she'd have trouble remembering to take her pills. But now, after ten months, it's _____ nature.

    a) first   b) second   c) third

6) Susan messed ____ and left the cookies in the oven for 25 minutes too long. They were ruined.

    a) up   b) over   c) away

7) Andrea didn't cheat. She won the election fair and _____.

    a) easily   b) circle   c) square

8) Bob didn't know anything about baking when he and Susan started selling cookies, but he quickly learned the _____.

    a) chains   b) ropes   c) strings

9) Ted and his friends were fooling ____ in the chemistry laboratory when they accidentally started a fire.

    a) around   b) about   c) away

10) Mary's daughter wanted the new Harry Potter book. But by the time they got to the bookstore, it was already sold ____.

    a) out   b) in   c) away

CROSSWORD PUZZLE

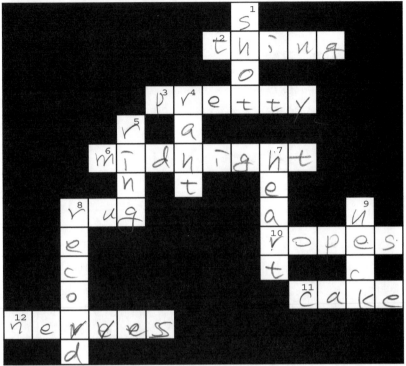

Across

2. Senator Brown's re-election would have been a sure ____ if he hadn't gotten caught stealing candy at Wal-Mart.
3. Chad is sitting _____. He just won the lottery.
6. Nicole had to burn the ____ oil to finish her English paper by the morning.
8. When Ted was caught copying his friend's math homework, his teacher wasn't willing to sweep it under the_____.
10. It takes time to learn the ___ when you start a new job.
11. Once you do it a few times, riding a unicycle is a piece of ___.
12. My friend's dog kept licking my hand. It was getting on my ____.

Down

1. Carla is a real big ____. She runs a large corporation.
4. Some people in restaurants like to ___ and rave when their soup is too cold.
5. I tried to give my friend a ____ this morning, but she wasn't home. I got her answering machine.
7. My ____ goes out to people who live in America, but don't speak any English.
8. Monica Lewinsky tried to set the_____ straight during her television interview with Barbara Walters.
9. Paying taxes every year is a pain in the _____.

ANSWERS TO REVIEW, pp. 164-165

SUSAN GETS A SURPRISE CALL

Donna from the National Cookie Company calls Susan. She wants to buy out Susan's Scrumptious Cookies. Susan is very happy.

Donna, de la National Cookie Company, llama a Susan. Quiere comprar la empresa de Susan's Scrumptious Cookies. Susan está muy contenta.

Susan: Hello?

Donna: Good afternoon. Are you Susan, of Susan's Scrumptious Cookies?

Susan: Yes, I am.

Donna: My name is Donna Jenkins, and I'm calling from the National Cookie Company. We're **nuts about** your cookies, and we'd like to sell them **all over** the country.

Susan: Unfortunately, we're running **on a shoestring** out of our kitchen. We can't make enough cookies for you.

Donna: My company wants to buy the recipe and the brand name from you.

Susan: Oh yeah? Why would you want to do that?

Donna: We have a successful **track record** of buying small companies and turning them into big ones.

Susan: **In that case**, I'm sure we can **come to an agreement**.

Donna: Great. You just **made my day**!

Susan: You'll need to **work out** the **nuts and bolts** of the agreement with my husband. He's the business manager.

Donna: May I speak with him now?

Susan: He's at a meeting. I'll have him get **in touch with** you when he returns.

Donna: Good. I **look forward to** speaking with him.

IDIOMS – LESSON 21

all over – throughout; everywhere
por todas partes

EXAMPLE 1: Nicole's classmates are from **all over** the world.
EXAMPLE 2: Oh no! I got ketchup **all over** my white sweater.

(to) come to an agreement – to reach an agreement
llegar a un acuerdo

EXAMPLE: If we can **come to an agreement** now, I can start work on Monday.

in that case – under that circumstance
en ese caso

EXAMPLE: It's snowing? **In that case**, you'd better take the bus to school today instead of driving.

(to be *or* to get) in touch with – to be *or* to get in contact with
en contacto con

EXAMPLE 1: I was surprised when Luis called me, since we hadn't been **in touch with** each other since high school.
EXAMPLE 2: Leave me your cell phone number, in case I need to **get in touch with** you while you're on vacation.

128

(to) look forward to – to anticipate eagerly
anticipar

EXAMPLE: I'm really **looking forward to** my trip to the Caribbean next winter.

(to) make one's day – to give one great satisfaction
darle una gran satisfacción, alegrarle el día a alguien

EXAMPLE: Our neighbors with the crazy dogs are moving away? That really **makes my day**!

(to be) nuts about – *Vea el capítulo 14*

nuts and bolts – details; basic components of something
detalles

EXAMPLE: I don't need to know the **nuts and bolts** of how the computer works — just show me how to turn it on.

SYNONYM: nitty-gritty. Example: Let's not get into the **nitty-gritty** of how the computer works. Just show me how to turn it on.

on a shoestring – on a very low budget
con muy poco dinero

EXAMPLE: Bob and Susan were living **on a shoestring** after Bob lost his job.

track record – a record of achievements or performances
historial, antecedentes

EXAMPLE: The women's basketball team at the University of Connecticut has an excellent **track record**.

(to) work out – to find a solution; to resolve
resolver

EXAMPLE: Nicole spent half the night helping Ted **work out** a very difficult chemistry problem.

NOTA: "Work out" tiene otros significados, incluyendo:
1. Desarrollar o formular. This plan won't **work out** — you'll need to go back to the drawing board and work out a new plan.
2. Tener éxito. Tony and Angela argue all the time. I don't think their marriage will **work out**.
3. Hacer ejercicio. After **working out** at the gym for two hours, Scott could barely walk.

✎ PRACTICE THE IDIOMS

Fill in the blank with the appropriate word:

1) There's a handsome exchange student from Costa Rica at Nicole's school this year. Nicole is nuts _____ him.

   a) with   b) into   c) about

2) Susan and Bob were able to come _____ an agreement with the representative from the National Cookie Company.

   a) from   b) with   c) to

3) When somebody has a successful track _____ , it's usually easy for them to find a new job.

   a) record   b) history   c) past

4) Let's have dinner on Saturday night. I'll get in touch ___ you later to choose a restaurant.

   a) from   b) by   c) with

5) Susan doesn't have a lot of money. In fact, she's running her business _____ a shoestring.

   a) with   b) on   c) in

6) You can find Starbucks coffee houses all _____ the country, from New York to California.

   a) over   b) above   c) within

7) Bob hasn't been on vacation in years. He's really looking _____ to his trip to Maine.

   a) above   b) forward   c) ahead

8) Ted's teacher helped him work _____ a study schedule.

   a) out   b) in   c) through

ANSWERS TO LESSON 21, p. 165

130

SUSAN SHARES THE GOOD NEWS

Bob tells Susan that the Village Market won't take their cookies anymore. Susan tells Bob that the National Cookie Company wants to buy out Susan's Scrumptious Cookies.

Bob le dice a Susan que el Village Market no va a volver a comprar sus galletas. Susan le dice a Bob que la National Cookie Company quiere comprar la empresa de Susan's Scrumptious Cookies.

Bob: Dear, I've got some bad news.

Susan: **What's the matter**, Bob?

Bob: The Village Market won't take any more of our cookies.

Susan: Why not? They're **selling like hotcakes**!

Bob: I know, but a lady found a blue hair in her cookie. Now Carol refuses to sell them.

Susan: Carol is such a **dragon lady**! We're **better off** having **nothing to do with her**.

Bob: She's not my **cup of tea** either, but she was selling lots of cookies.

Susan: Oh well. **That's the way the cookie crumbles**. Ha ha. **Get it?**

Bob: Susan, this is **no laughing matter**!

Susan: Bob, we don't need the Village Market anymore.

Bob: Why not?

Susan: The National Cookie Company called. They want to **buy out** our business.

Bob: Susan, this is a **dream come true**. **It looks like** we've **struck it rich**!

Susan: Yes. Soon we'll be **rolling in dough**!

IDIOMS – LESSON 22

better off – in a more fortunate position
mejor

EXAMPLE: We're **better off** leaving for France on Thursday evening, so we can spend the entire weekend there.

NOTA: Use la forma del gerundio (-ing) con el verbo que siga a "better off".

(to) buy out – to purchase an entire business or someone's share of a business
comprar una empresa o la parte de un socio

EXAMPLE: Microsoft told Mike they'd like to **buy out** his company for 12 million dollars.

---

cup of tea – *Vea el capítulo 5*

---

dragon lady – a nasty woman who misuses her power
una mujer desagradable que abusa de su poder

EXAMPLE: Beth is a real **dragon lady**. She's always screaming at her employees and blaming them for her mistakes. I hope she gets fired!

SYNONYMS: bitch [grosero]; shrew

(to) get it – to understand
entender

EXAMPLE: I invited 40 people to my Thanksgiving dinner, but only 10 people came. I don't **get it**!

---

it looks like – it's likely that
parece probable

EXAMPLE: **It looks like** I'll be able to get out of work early today, so let's plan on meeting downtown at 4:30.

---

no laughing matter – nothing to joke about; something serious
no es broma, va en serio

EXAMPLE: When the hurricane came into town, it was **no laughing matter**.
SYNONYM: no joke

---

nothing to do with (someone *or* something) – not have any relationship with someone; to not get involved with something
no tener nada que ver con (alguien)

EXAMPLE: They used to be friends, but now Nicole wants **nothing to do with** Andrea.

---

rolling in dough – very rich
muy rico

EXAMPLE: Susan and Bob don't need to work anymore. They're **rolling in dough**.

NOTA: Éste es un juego de palabras. "Dough" quiere decir "dinero" además de "masa". The dough (cookies) made by Bob and Susan brought them much dough (money).
SYNONYMS: rolling in it; rolling in money; loaded

(to) sell like hot cakes – *Vea el capítulo 17*

(to) strike it rich – to attain sudden financial success
tener un golpe de fortuna, conseguir mucho dinero de repente

EXAMPLE: Chad **struck it rich** with the winning lottery ticket.

---

that's the way the cookie crumbles – that's the way things go sometimes and there's nothing you can do about it
así es la vida

EXAMPLE: You lost your job? **That's the way the cookie crumbles**.
SYNONYM: that's life. Example: I'm sorry to hear that you lost your job, but **that's life**!

What's the matter? – *Vea el capítulo 2*

Choose the best substitute for the phrase or sentence in bold:

1) **"What's the matter**? You don't look happy."
   a) How are you?
   b) What does it mean?
   c) What's wrong?

2) We sold our business. Now **we're rolling in dough**!
   a) we're still making cookies
   b) we're rich
   c) we're poor

3) How could a woman find a hair in her cookie? **I just don't get it**.
   a) I don't understand it.
   b) I don't get hair in my cookies.
   c) I don't believe it.

4) Ted and Amber think they're going to **strike it rich** in the music business.
   a) get hurt
   b) make lots of money
   c) hit something

5) Bob thought that losing his job at the furniture store was **no laughing matter**.
   a) something serious
   b) something to laugh about
   c) something that doesn't really matter

6) My boss at the plastics company was a real **dragon lady**. Whenever I went into her office, she started yelling.
   a) ugly woman
   b) nasty woman
   c) fire-breathing monster

7) Nicole, I'm sorry you lost the election for president, but **that's the way the cookie crumbles**.
   a) that's how it goes and you can't do anything about it
   b) sometimes cookies fall apart
   c) when bad things happen, you should be very upset

8) A few months after Peter fired Bob, his furniture store **went out of business**.
   a) started doing better
   b) moved to a different location
   c) closed

ANSWERS TO LESSON 22, p. 165

BOB HAS A SURPRISE VISITOR

Bob's former boss Peter, from the furniture store, comes to visit.
He offers Bob his old job back, but Bob's not interested.

El ex-jefe de Bob, Peter, el de la tienda de muebles, viene de
visita. Le vuelve a ofrecer a Bob su antiguo trabajo, pero a Bob
no le interesa.

Peter: Hi Bob. I was just in the neighborhood so I thought I'd **stop by**.

Bob: **Come on in**. Take a cookie.

Peter: Thanks. I'm glad to see you're not **holding a grudge against** me for firing you.

Bob: Not at all. **At first**, it **burned me up**. But I feel better now.

Peter: Good. I'm glad you have **no hard feelings**. How would you like your old job back?

Bob: What happened to your wonderful new manager?

Peter: She drank at work. By five o'clock, she'd be lying under a dining room table, **three sheets to the wind**. Yesterday, I finally **got rid of** her.

Bob: Let me **get this straight**. You replaced me with some crazy woman who **got plastered** every day **on the job**?

Peter: Yes. I **lost my head**.

137

Bob: I don't think you lost your head. I just think you've got rocks in your head!

Peter: Bob, I'm trying to **level with you**. I never should've **let you go**.

Bob: **No use crying over spilt milk.**

Peter: So you'll come back and work for me?

Bob: **Not on your life!** Susan and I are very **well off** now. We just sold our new company for a **small fortune**!

IDIOMS – LESSON 23

at first – *Vea el capítulo 16*

(to) burn someone up – to make someone angry
molestar o enojar a alguien

EXAMPLE: Jenny didn't vote for Nicole. That really **burns Nicole up**.

come on in – enter
entre, pase

EXAMPLE: **Come on in**, the door's open!

(to) get plastered [slang] – to get drunk
emborracharse

EXAMPLE: Rob **got plastered** at the wedding and fell into the wedding cake.

SYNONYMS: to get loaded [slang]; to get sloshed [slang]

(to) get rid of – to free oneself of; to dispose of
librarse de

EXAMPLE: We finally **got rid of** our spider problem, but now we have ants.

(to) get (something) straight – to clarify; to understand
entender bien, aclarar (algo)

EXAMPLE: Are you sure you **got the directions straight**?

(to) hold a grudge against (someone) – to stay angry with someone about a past offense
tenerle rencor a alguien

EXAMPLE: Nicole **holds a grudge against Jenny** for voting for Andrea instead of her.

(to) let (someone) go – to fire; dismiss employees
despedir a alguien

EXAMPLE: The investment bank **let Chris go** after they discovering he was stealing erasers, paper clips, and other office supplies.

(to) level with (someone) – to speak openly and honestly with someone
confiar en (alguien), hablar honestamente

EXAMPLE: Let me **level with you**: I'm voting for Andrea instead of you.

(to) lose one's head – to lose control of one's behavior; to not know what one is doing
perder control del comportamiento, perder la cabeza (lit.)

EXAMPLE: Nicole **lost her head** after losing the elections and started yelling at all her friends.

SYNONYM: To lose it. Example: When Lisa's boyfriend broke up with her, she started screaming at him right in the restaurant. She really **lost it**!

no hard feelings – no anger; no bitterness
no tener rencor

EXAMPLE: After the elections, Andrea said to Nicole, "I hope there are **no hard feelings**."

no use crying over spilt milk – there's no point in regretting something that's too late to change
no tiene remedio; a lo hecho, pecho

EXAMPLE: Nicole realized she'd made some mistakes with her campaign for president, but there was **no use crying over spilt milk**.

Not on your life! – definitely not
¡De ninguna manera!

EXAMPLE: You want me to sit in that hot sauna for an hour? **Not on your life**!

SYNONYMS: No way! Nothing doing! Not a chance!

on the job – at work
en el trabajo

EXAMPLE: Jennifer has four men **on the job** painting her house.

small fortune – a good amount of money
una buena cantidad de dinero, una pequeña fortuna (lit.)

EXAMPLE: When her great aunt died, Anne inherited a **small fortune**.

(to) stop by – to pay a quick visit
visitar, pasar a ver

EXAMPLE: I'm having some friends over for pizza tomorrow night. Why don't you **stop by**?

three sheets to the wind – drunk
borracho como una cuba

EXAMPLE: After drinking four margaritas, Ellen was **three sheets to the wind**.

SYNONYMS: wasted [slang]; liquored up [slang]; dead drunk

well off – wealthy
rico

EXAMPLE: Betsy's grandfather, Herbert Snippinger, used to be very **well off**, but he lost most of his fortune when the U.S. stock market crashed in 1929.

✒ PRACTICE THE IDIOMS

Choose the best substitute for the phrase or sentence in bold:

1) Nicole was very angry that she lost the election. Her mother told her **there was no use crying over spilt milk**.
   a) there was no point in feeling bad about what can't be changed
   b) she should think about all the mistakes she made
   c) maybe she could still change the results

2) Many people have died while climbing Mount Everest. Would I like to try it? **Not on your life!**
   a) Not if it means you'll be risking your life!
   b) Yes, definitely
   c) No way!

3) When Carol told Bob she could no longer sell Susan's Scrumptious Cookies, it really **burned him up.**
   a) made him feel happy
   b) made him feel sick
   c) made him very angry

4) Sara, I'm going to have to **let you go.** You come to work late every day and spend all day chatting with your friends.
   a) fire you
   b) give you more vacation time
   c) yell at you

5) One day, Nicole woke up with big red spots on her face. She didn't know how to **get rid of** them.
   a) make more of
   b) remove
   c) encourage

6) Thanks for coming to my party. **Come on in!**
   a) See you later!
   b) Go away!
   c) Enter!

7) Susan was **three sheets to the wind.** Bob told her not to drink any more piña coladas.
   a) really drunk
   b) very thirsty
   c) feeling very tired

8) Now that Bob is **well off**, he definitely won't be taking a job at McDonald's.
   a) employed
   b) feeling well
   c) wealthy

ANSWERS TO LESSON 23, p. 165

AMBER WRITES A SONG

Ted always writes the songs for the rock band. But now Amber says she wants to start writing songs too. She sings him the first lines of her new song.

Ted siempre escribe las canciones del grupo de rock. Pero ahora Amber dice que ella también quiere empezar a escribir canciones. Le canta las primeras estrofas de su nueva canción.

Amber: Ted, you know how **all along** you've been **in charge of** all the lyrics for our band?

Ted: That's right, Amber. Everybody loves my songs!

Amber: Well, I hope they'll love my songs too.

Ted: But you don't write songs.

Amber: I'm **sick and tired of** singing your songs all the time. I want to sing my own songs!

Ted: Okay, no need to **freak out**! **First things first**. Have you written a song yet?

Amber: Yes, **as a matter of fact**, I have.

Ted: Well, let's hear it then.

Amber: Okay, but it's still a work **in progress**.

Ted: Stop trying to **buy time**. Let's hear the song!

Amber: ♪ My boyfriend is crazy. **Crazy about** baking cookies.
           I know **for sure** that there is no cure... ♪

Ted: **Cut it out**! Stop teasing me. I *am* cured.

Amber: **All better**?

Ted: Yes. I'll never bake another cookie again. My parents
           made a fortune. Now we can all just **chill out**!

IDIOMS – LESSON 24

all along – throughout; from beginning to end
todo el tiempo, desde el principio hasta el final

EXAMPLE: Jenny told Nicole she would vote for her, but **all along** she
was planning on voting for Andrea.

all better – completely cured
completamente curado

EXAMPLE: "**All better**?" asked Nancy, after her son stopped crying.

as a matter of fact – *Vea el capítulo 20*

(to) buy time – to make more time available (in order to
achieve a certain purpose)
hacer más tiempo disponible, ganar tiempo

EXAMPLE: We're not sure yet whether or not we want to buy the house.
We'd better **buy some time** so we can think about it over the weekend.

(to) chill out [slang] – to relax
calmarse, relajarse

EXAMPLE: **Chill out**! If we miss this train, we'll just take the next one.

(to be) crazy about – *Vea el capítulo 5*

(to) cut it out – stop it; stop the annoying behavior
dejar de

EXAMPLE: Tracy was chewing gum loudly during the movie. Her boyfriend finally told her to **cut it out**.

first things first – let's focus on the most important thing or task first
lo primero es lo primero

EXAMPLE: "You want to work here at Lulu's Dance Club? **First things first**, have you ever worked as a dancer before?"

for sure – *Vea el capítulo 19*

(to) freak out [slang] – to respond to something irrationally or crazily; to overreact
reaccionar de forma irracional

EXAMPLE: Ashley's parents **freaked out** when she told them she was dropping out of college to become an actress.

(to be) in charge of – having responsibility for
a cargo de

EXAMPLE: Justin has an important job. He's **in charge of** all international sales for his company.

in progress – happening; under way
en progreso

EXAMPLE: The play is already **in progress**, so you'll have to wait until intermission to sit down.

(to) make a fortune – to make a lot of money
ganar una fortuna

EXAMPLE: Mike **made a fortune** when he sold his company to Microsoft.
SYNONYMS: to make a bundle; to make a killing

(to be) sick and tired of – completely bored with; sick of
harto de

EXAMPLE: Ted is **sick and tired of** hearing about what an excellent student Nicole is.
SYNONYM: (to be) fed up with. Example: Joan's husband spent all weekend playing cards with his friends. She's **fed up with** him!

✎ PRACTICE THE IDIOMS

Fill in the blanks using these idioms:

buy time	**cut it out**
chill out	**in charge of**
freaked out	**sick and tired of**
all along	**first things first**

1) Nicole really _____ when she heard she lost the presidential election. She threw her books across the room!

2) Ted, why do you always leave your dirty clothes on the floor? Your mother is _____ cleaning up after you.

3) Donna, from the National Cookie Company, wanted Susan to sign a contract right away. Susan told her _____. She wanted to speak to a lawyer before signing any papers.

4) As president of the Spanish Club, Nicole will be _____ organizing a trip to Spain in the spring.

5) When Nicole saw a group of her brother's friends laughing at her, she told them to _____.

6) After losing the election, Nicole was very upset. She needed to take it easy and _____.

7) Bob and Susan weren't sure yet how much they wanted to sell their cookie company for. They needed to _____ so they could get some advice.

8) Nicole had assumed _____ that she was going to win the election. She was really surprised when she lost.

BONUS PRACTICE

Fill in the blank with the missing word:

1) Billy fell down the stairs and started crying. When he finally stopped, his mother asked, "All _____?"

   a) good   b) better   c) okay

2) Amber was happy when Ted said they didn't have to bake any more cookies. She was sick and tired ___ baking cookies.

   a) of   b) with   c) at

3) David hasn't yet made up his mind whether or not to accept the job offer. He needs to _____ more time.

   a) buy   b) purchase   c) get

4) The man behind me on the train was whistling loudly. It was giving me a headache. Finally, I told him to __ it out.

   a) stop   b) cut   c) sever

5) Chill ___! We're only going to be a few minutes late.

   a) it   b) in   c) out

6) Carlos ____ a fortune working in computers in the late 90's. He was able to retire at age 39.

   a) had   b) made   c) found

7) The students were told that while the test was __ progress, they wouldn't be allowed to leave the classroom.

   a) with   b) in   c) at

8) Victoria has a big job. She's in charge ___ the marketing department at her company.

   a) at   b) with   c) of

ANSWERS TO LESSON 24, p. 166

TED BRINGS HOME MORE GOOD NEWS

Ted tells his family that a talent agent wants to meet with him. The agent will fly Ted and Amber to New York. Nicole announces that she's been named president of the Spanish Club.

Ted le dice a su familia que un agente buscador de talentos quiere reunirse con él. El agente les pagará el viaje a Nueva York a Ted y a Amber. Nicole anuncia que ha sido nombrada presidenta del Club de Español.

Ted: Amber and I are going to **break into** the music business. Last night after our concert, a talent agent asked us to meet with him in New York.

Susan: Congratulations! We'll give you some **spending money** for your trip.

Ted: No need. The agent is **footing the bill** for everything. And when we get there, he's going to **wine and dine** us.

Susan: He must think you're the **cream of the crop**.

Ted: He thinks we sound like the Goo Goo Dolls.

Nicole: Who are they?

Ted: You're really **out of it**. They're a popular rock band.

Nicole: Our family is certainly on a **winning streak**. I was elected president of the Spanish Club today.

Ted: The Spanish Club? **Big deal!**

Nicole: You don't **get it**, Ted. This is only the beginning. Today, president of the Spanish Club. Tomorrow, ambassador to Spain!

Ted: Well, Ambassador, you'll need to **wrap up** my chemistry homework before you leave for the Spanish Embassy.

Susan: A rock star and a diplomat — I'm so proud of both of you!

IDIOMS – LESSON 25

Big deal! – So what? That doesn't really matter
¿Y qué?, no importa

EXAMPLE: You won five dollars in the lottery? **Big deal!**

NOTA: También existe la expresión "it's no big deal". Example: Don't worry about losing the book I lent you. **It's no big deal.**

(to) break into – to enter or be let into a profession
meterse en (una profesión)

EXAMPLE: If you want to **break into** journalism, it's a good idea to work on a college newspaper.

NOTA: "Break into" tiene otros significados:
1. Interrumpir. Robert and I were talking. Please don't try to **break into** our conversation.
2. Entrar a la fuerza. Somebody **broke into** Peter's house and stole his DVD player.
3. Empezar algo de repente. After receiving the check from the National Cookie Company, Susan **broke into** song.

cream of the crop – the best of a group
lo mejor de un grupo

EXAMPLE: In the world of women's tennis, the Williams sisters are the **cream of the crop.**

(to) foot the bill – to pay the bill
pagar la cuenta

EXAMPLE: You paid last time we went out for dinner. Let me **foot the bill** this time.

SYNONYM: to pick up the tab. Example: Do you mind **picking up the tab** this time? I paid last time.

(to) get it – *Vea el capítulo 21*

(to be) out of it – not aware or knowledgeable about trends or modern habits
no enterarse de modas o costumbres modernas

EXAMPLE: Don't ask for Susan's advice on fashion. She's really **out of it**. She wears sneakers with everything.

NOTA: "Out of it" también quiere decir "confuso" o "desorientado". Example: After staying up all night practicing guitar, Ted felt really **out of it** the next day.

spending money - money for minor expenses
dinero de bolsillo

EXAMPLE: Before Tim left for Europe, his parents gave him $400 **spending money**.

SYNONYM: pocket money

(to) wine and dine – to take someone out for an evening or an expensive meal
agasajar

EXAMPLE: Donna **wined and dined** Bob and Susan and then presented them with a contract for the sale of Susan's Scrumptious Cookies.

(to be on a) winning streak – a series of wins
buena racha

EXAMPLE: The basketball team hasn't lost a game all season. They're on a **winning streak**!

(to) wrap up – to finish
terminar

EXAMPLE: **If you wrap up** your homework by 8 p.m., we'll have time to catch a movie tonight.

✍ PRACTICE THE IDIOMS

Fill in the blank with the missing word:

1) I invited you to dinner, so let me _____ the bill.

   a) hand off   b) arm   c) foot

2) My friend Kate is really _____ it. She doesn't even know who Oprah Winfrey is.

   a) out of   b) into   c) unaware of

3) Ted told Amber he'd need to call her back later in the evening since he was just _____ to have dinner.

   a) up   b) around   c) about

4) After Bob and Susan wrap ___ the sale of their business, they can relax for a while.

   a) through   b) around   c) up

5) Sally got a job with a law firm in Manhattan? ___ deal!

   a) Small   b) Big   c) Huge

6) We love to visit our friends in Santiago, Chile. They always _____ and dine us.

   a) liquor   b) wine   c) beer

7) Bob and Susan plan to give Nicole $1,000 per year of spending _____ when she's in college.

   a) cash   b) dough   c) money

8) I recommend you go to a concert at Carnegie Hall. The musicians who play there are always the cream of the _____.

   a) crop   b) lawn   c) lot

ANSWERS TO LESSON 25, p. 166

Review for Lessons 21-25

Fill in the blank with the missing word:

1) Next year, Ted will be traveling all ____ the world with his band.

   a) about   b) inside   c) over

2) After his fifth vodka, Steve was ____ sheets to the wind.

   a) five   b) three   c) two

3) For a while, the Johnsons were living _____ a shoestring. They couldn't afford to eat out at restaurants.

   a) with   b) on   c) by

4) When my friend lost her favorite necklace, I told her it was no use crying over spilt _____.

   a) milk   b) juice   c) beer

5) Joel has a fun job. He's ___ charge of advertising sales for *Mad,* the best humor magazine in America.

   a) at   b) on   c) in

6) Please put away your wallet! Let me ___ the bill.

   a) arm   b) foot   c) hand

7) My friend was running around like a chicken with its head cut off. I told her to chill _____.

   a) out   b) in   c) down

8) Bob worked out the nuts and ____ of the agreement with the National Cookie Company.

   a) details   b) bolts   c) tacks

9) After Martha's neighbor chopped down her apple tree, she held a grudge ____ him for years.

    a) from   b) against   c) for

10) I arrived late to the stadium. The baseball game was already ____ progress.

    a) through   b) in   c) at

11) My friend invited me out for a drink, but I told her I'd first need to wrap ____ some things at the office.

    a) through   b) along   c) up

12) I'm ____ and tired of telemarketers calling me in the evening trying to sell my stuff I don't want.

    a) sick   b) ill   c) angry

13) Kristen's boss paid her a compliment. He said she was the best salesperson in the company. That really ____ her day.

    a) made   b) created   c) ruined

14) The person seated behind me on the airplane kept on kicking my seat. Finally, I told him to ____ it out.

    a) stop   b) cut   c) fly

15) Amber hopes to break ____ the modeling business after she graduates from high school. She can definitely model nose rings and tattoos!

    a) into   b) in   c) around

CROSSWORD PUZZLE

Across

1. First things ___. Before we start wandering around the streets of Paris, let's look at a map and plan our route.
3. The company will wine and ___ their top candidates for this position.
5. Nicole was really looking ____ to her school trip to Spain.
7. Bob is an engineer. He tries to understand the nuts and _____ of how things work.
9. When the stock market collapsed, Bob lost his ___ and sold everything.
10. Nicole's boyfriend forgot his wallet, so she had to foot the ___ .
11. Bob no longer shops at the Village Market. He holds a _____ against them.
13. I was sick and ____ of watching my colleague flirt with her boss.

Down

2. We can't afford a new computer for the office. We're running on a ____.
3. Bette Davis may have been a great actress, but she was a _____ lady in real life.
4. The musicians from the Juilliard School of Music are the cream of the _____.
6. Diane and Mike just bought a mansion. They're rolling in _____.
8. Mary left her husband George for a younger man. She told George, "I hope there are no ____ feelings about this."
12. Stephen King has a long track ____ of writing bestsellers.

ANSWERS TO REVIEW, p. 166

VOCABULARIO ÚTIL DE LOS DIÁLOGOS

advertising campaign	campaña publicitaria
agreement	acuerdo, contrato
argue	discutir
audience	público
awake	despierto
bake	asar al horno
bet	apostar
bunch	ramo, puñado, racimo
brand name	marca
chewy	como chicle
choice	opción
competition	competición
count	contar
cured	curado
customers	clientes
demand	exigir
dye	tinte, teñir
election	elecciones
enjoy	disfrutar
fault	culpa
fired	despedido
furniture	muebles
grades	notas
gross	asqueroso
hairstyle	peinado
helper	ayudante
hire	alquilar, contratar
imagine	imaginar
in the meantime	mientras tanto
ingredients	ingredientes
instead of	en vez de

jealous	celoso
kiss	beso, besar
lyrics	letra (de una canción)
mall	centro comercial
manage	manejar, controlar
marry	casarse
meanwhile	mientras tanto
mind	mente
move into	mudarse a
musician	músico
naked	desnudo
neighborhood	vecindario, barrio
nonsense	tontería
perform	realizar, actuar
prepared to	preparado para
promise	prometer, promesa
re-count	recuento
recipe	receta
refuse	negarse a
replace	reemplazar, reponer
rock band	grupo de rock
run a business	llevar un negocio
scrumptious	delicioso
slave	esclavo
speech	discurso
tent	tienda de campaña
vote	voto, votar
vote for	votar por
wonderful	maravilloso
yum-yum	delicioso

RESPUESTAS ~ ANSWER KEY

LESSON 1: BOB'S DAY AT WORK
1. b   5. b
2. a   6. a
3. c   7. c
4. a   8. c

LESSON 2: BOB RETURNS HOME WITH BAD NEWS
1. c   5. a
2. b   6. c
3. c   7. a
4. c   8. b

LESSON 3: TED'S DAY AT SCHOOL
1. c   5. c
2. a   6. a
3. a   7. b
4. b   8. a

LESSON 4: NICOLE'S DAY AT SCHOOL
1. b   5. c
2. c   6. a
3. b   7. c
4. b   8. a

BONUS PRACTICE
1. c   4. b
2. a   5. c
3. b   6. b

LESSON 5: TED GOES OUT FOR THE EVENING
1. b   5. a
2. a   6. b
3. c   7. b
4. b   8. c

REVIEW: LESSONS 1-5

1. b	5. b	9. c	13. c
2. b	6. a	10. a	14. b
3. c	7. b	11. b	15. b
4. c	8. c	12. a	

LESSON 6: SUSAN STAYS HOME & BAKES COOKIES

1. a	5. b
2. b	6. b
3. c	7. a
4. c	8. a

LESSON 7: SUSAN HIRES BOB TO RUN HER BUSINESS

1. b	5. b
2. a	6. c
3. c	7. a
4. a	8. c

LESSON 8: TED FORMS A ROCK BAND

1. a	5. b
2. a	6. b
3. c	7. b
4. a	8. c

LESSON 9: NICOLE FOR PRESIDENT!

1. b	5. a
2. a	6. c
3. b	7. b
4. c	8. a

LESSON 10: BOB VISITS THE VILLAGE MARKET

1. c	5. a
2. b	6. a
3. a	7. c
4. b	8. a

REVIEW: LESSONS 6-10

1. c	5. b	9. b
2. a	6. a	10. b
3. c	7. c	
4. b	8. a	

160

LESSON 11: BOB DRIVES A HARD BARGAIN

Abe: Hi, Jeff. <u>How's it going</u>?

Jeff: Fine, thanks. I've only scheduled a half hour for this meeting, so we better <u>get the ball rolling</u>.

Abe: Jeff, I need you to come up with a new advertising campaign for my furniture shop.

Jeff: I've had a chance to <u>crunch some numbers</u>, and you'll need to pay me $30,000 to come up with some new ideas.

Abe: Thirty thousand dollars? That's really <u>out of the question!</u>

Jeff: Listen, Abe, I need to <u>make a living</u> too. I've got a wife and seven children at home.

Abe: I'll pay you $20,000.

Jeff: If you want quality work, you have to pay for it. Let's say $25,000?

Abe: Okay, okay. You've <u>twisted my arm</u>. I'll pay you $23,000.

Jeff: <u>Now you're talking</u>. That's a fair price.

Abe: You certainly <u>drive a hard bargain</u>.

Jeff: I know, but you'll be happy with my work.

161

LESSON 12: BOB'S BIG COOKIE ORDER

1. a	5. b
2. b	6. c
3. a	7. a
4. b	8. c

BONUS PRACTICE

1. c	4. a
2. a	5. b
3. c	6. b

LESSON 13: AMBER COMES OVER TO BAKE COOKIES

1. c	5. b
2. c	6. a
3. a	7. a
4. b	8. b

LESSON 14: AMBER AND TED HEAT UP THE KITCHEN

I met Bob in college. He was in my English Literature class. I liked him right away. For me, it was love at first sight. I wrote him several love poems, though I never gave them to him. Then I found out he had a girlfriend. I saw him making out with a girl named Joyce. It looked like she was crazy about Bob too. But later that week, I heard that she was a nasty person and that she treated him like dirt. So I decided to go ahead and ask him to the movies. He said he was too busy. It was crunch time, and he had to crank out a paper for literature class and study for several exams. But I didn't give up. I kept plugging away. Then one day he broke up with Joyce and asked me out to dinner. That was 25 years ago, and we're still together. Fortunately, we're still head over heels in love with each other!

LESSON 15: NICOLE PRACTICES HER ELECTION SPEECH

1. b	5. b
2. a	6. b
3. c	7. c
4. a	8. a

REVIEW: LESSONS 11-15

1. a	5. a	9. b
2. c	6. a	10. b
3. b	7. b	11. b
4. c	8. c	12. a

LESSON 16: BOB BRINGS THE COOKIES TO THE VILLAGE MARKET

1. b	5. b
2. b	6. a
3. c	7. b
4. c	8. c

LESSON 17: CAROL TELLS BOB THE GOOD NEWS

1. a	5. b
2. b	6. c
3. a	7. a
4. b	8. c

LESSON 18: EVERYONE BAKES COOKIES

1. c	5. b
2. b	6. c
3. c	7. a
4. a	8. b

BONUS PRACTICE

1. c	5. b
2. a	6. a
3. c	7. c
4. b	8. b

LESSON 19: NICOLE'S CLOSE ELECTION

Ted: Nicole, my teacher gave me back my chemistry homework. I got a terrible grade! I thought <u>for sure</u> you'd help me get an A+.

Nicole: I'm sorry. I really did <u>give it my best shot</u>, but I guess it wasn't good enough.

Ted: Not good enough? That's right. You really <u>messed up</u>!

Nicole: You never should've asked me to do your homework. Don't try to <u>put the blame on me</u> for your bad grades.

Ted: Yes, my mistake. I thought you were a <u>sure thing</u>!

Nicole: So you'll get a bad grade in chemistry. Just learn to <u>live with it</u>. Here, take one of Mom's cookies. It'll help <u>cheer you up</u>.

Ted: You think a stupid cookie will cheer me up? <u>Give me a break</u>!

LESSON 20: BOB GETS AN ANGRY CALL FROM CAROL

1. a	5. b
2. b	6. c
3. a	7. b
4. c	8. b

REVIEW: LESSONS 16-20

1. c	5. b	9. a
2. b	6. a	10. a
3. c	7. c	
4. a	8. b	

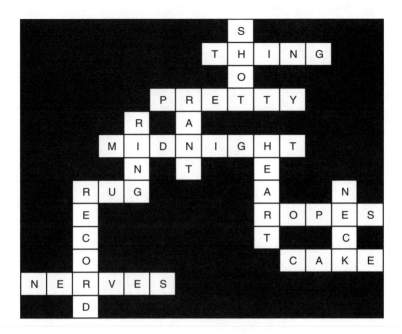

LESSON 21: SUSAN GETS A SURPRISE CALL
1. c   5. b
2. c   6. a
3. a   7. b
4. c   8. a

LESSON 22: SUSAN SHARES THE GOOD NEWS
1. c   5. a
2. b   6. b
3. a   7. a
4. b   8. c

LESSON 23: BOB HAS A SURPRISE VISITOR
1. a   5. b
2. c   6. c
3. c   7. a
4. a   8. c

LESSON 24: AMBER WRITES A SONG

1. freaked out
2. sick and tired of
3. first things first
4. in charge of
5. cut it out
6. chill out
7. buy time
8. all along

BONUS PRACTICE

1. b
2. a
3. a
4. b
5. c
6. b
7. b
8. c

LESSON 25: TED BRINGS HOME MORE GOOD NEWS

1. c
2. a
3. c
4. c
5. b
6. b
7. c
8. a

REVIEW: LESSONS 21-25

1. c
2. b
3. b
4. a
5. c
6. b
7. a
8. b
9. b
10. b
11. c
12. a
13. a
14. b
15. a

ÍNDICE ALFABÉTICO
INDEX

170

ORDER FORM
Language Success Press
2232 S. Main St. #345
Ann Arbor, MI 48103
sales@languagesuccesspress.com
www.languagesuccesspress.com
fax: (303) 484-2004

Speak English Like An American for Native Spanish Speakers...$24.95 (includes book & audio CD)

TITLE	Quantity	Line total
Speak English Like An American: book & CD...$24.95		
Speak English Like An American: CD only.........$9.95		
Subtotal		
Shipment to Michigan Add 6% Sales Tax		
Shipping (see below)		
TOTAL		

U.S. Shipping Charges: $4.95 for orders up to $25. $6.95 for orders $25.01-$50. $8.95 for orders $50.01-$100. $10.95 for orders $100.01-$200. Add an additional $2 for each additional $100 or part thereof. **International Shipping Charges:** Canada & Mexico: Multiply the U.S. shipping rate by 1.5. Overseas Shipping: Multipy the U.S. shipping rate by 2.

SHIP TO:

Name_____

Institution_____

Address_____

City_____State_____

Zip_____Country_____

E-mail address_____

Order online at: www.languagesuccesspress.com

Visite nuestro sitio web, donde encontrará:

- Un formulario de pedido en línea
- Enlaces interesantes
- La receta secreta de "Susan's Scrumptious Cookies"

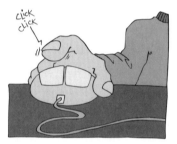

www.languagesuccesspress.com